CHOICES AND CONSEQUENCES

CHOICES AND CONSEQUENCES

Contemporary Policy Issues in Education

Edited by
Ronald G. Ehrenberg

ILR Press
Ithaca, New York

Library of Congress Cataloging-in-Publication Data

Choices and consequences : contemporary policy issues in education /
    edited by Ronald G. Ehrenberg.
        p.   cm.
    Includes bibliographical references.
    ISBN 0-87546-333-9 (acid-free paper)
    1. College choice—United States.   2. College majors—United
States.   3. Higher education and state—United States.
I. Ehrenberg, Ronald G.
LB2350.5.C56   1994
378.73—dc20   94-31499

Copies of this book may be ordered through bookstores or directly
from

ILR Press
School of Industrial and Labor Relations
Cornell University
Ithaca, NY 14853-3901
607/255-2264

Printed on acid-free recycled paper in the United States of America

5   4   3   2   1

Contents

Tables and Figures

FIGURES

CHOICES AND CONSEQUENCES

Choices in Education
Ronald G. Ehrenberg

The American educational system consumed over 7.5 percent of our gross domestic product in 1992. In that year, over 47 million students were enrolled in elementary and secondary schools and over 14 million students in institutions of higher education. By far, the vast majority of students at all levels attend public institutions, and educational expenditures represented almost 35 percent of all expenditures of state and local governments in the early 1990s (National Center for Education Statistics [NCES] 1992, Tables 1, 31, 35).

Increasingly, this large sector of our economy has come under intense scrutiny. For example, at the elementary and secondary levels, critics point to declining test scores and continued high dropout rates—the latter being of special concern for low-income and minority students— even though real per student expenditures on elementary and secondary education increased by 58 percent over the 1970–71 to 1991–92 period (NCES 1992, Tables 3, 31, 38).

To take another example: Increasing foreign competition and the growing earnings differentials between college-educated and lesser-educated workers suggest both the importance of a highly skilled, educated workforce for our economy and the increased incentives for individuals

The four chapters in this volume were originally presented at the Contemporary Policy Issues in Education conference, which was held at Cornell University on May 21, 1993 and was jointly sponsored by the ILR-Cornell Institute for Labor Market Policies and the Princeton University Industrial Relations Section. The conference was organized by Orley Ashenfelter of Princeton and myself. It was attended by approximately fifty individuals spanning academia, private foundations, nonprofit research organizations, and public school systems. The authors of the papers benefitted from both the general discussion at the conference and the detailed comments of the assigned discussants. The latter included Orley Ashenfelter, Alan Krueger, and David Card of Princeton; Richard Murnane and Ronald Ferguson of Harvard; John Abowd and Maria Hanratty of Cornell; and William Spriggs of the Economic Policy Institute.

to obtain higher education. Yet these incentives are present at a time when many people are concerned that the higher education sector is not performing efficiently and that tuition levels at private institutions are soaring out of sight. Tuition levels at public institutions have also grown rapidly, partly because of diminished levels of state support.

Society has high expectations for our educational system, and social science research should contribute to helping meet these expectations. Research on the choices that participants in the system make, and on the consequences of these choices, is particularly useful and often provides information that is directly relevant to the policy debate. Thus the four chapters in this volume all address the choices, and the consequences of choices, made by students, teachers, and school administrators. They are grouped together in this book in the belief that providing them this way will increase their influence on public policy.

The first two chapters deal with the characteristics of teachers in American public elementary and secondary schools. Of concern to policy-makers are three primary questions: how to assure a flow of people into the teaching profession in the face of large numbers of expected retire-ments in the decade ahead; how to assure an adequate flow of math and science teachers particularly; and how to maintain or increase teachers' quality.

Eric Hanushek and Richard Pace's paper first compares the academic test scores of people entering teaching with the test scores of all high school graduates. Their research is motivated by studies that show that high school seniors who plan to become teachers disproportionately score in the lower half of the test distribution of all high school students who plan to enter college. This finding, coupled with a set of previous studies that show that teachers' test scores appear to be positively associated with the amount that their students learn, would seem to argue for some action to increase teacher quality, as measured by test scores.

Hanushek and Pace's important observation is that the people who actually enter teaching are not the same people who initially express interest in becoming teachers. Many who express interest never com-plete teacher education programs or find employment in education. Using longitudinal data from the High School and Beyond survey—a national sample of high school seniors in 1980 who were followed through the spring of 1986—they find that those initially interested in teaching who drop out along the way or fail to find employment as teachers tend to be lower-ability students (although the authors point out some important differences across gender, race, and ethnic groups). Moreover, many people who enter teaching upon graduation from college are not among the set of people who initially plan to be teachers, and members of this former group tend to be higher-ability students than the people who initially express interest in teaching.

As a result, they find that, on average, people who are employed as teachers within six years of graduating high school tend to have substantially higher test scores than those who express interest in teaching as a career while in high school. Hanushek and Pace caution, however, as did Orley Ashenfelter in his conference comments, that, on average, new teachers' test scores are lower than those of typical college graduates. So although the test scores of people entering teaching are not as low as some might think, they also are not as high as others might have hoped.

The second part of the Hanushek and Pace paper addresses policies aimed at increasing the flow of college graduates into teaching careers. Specifically, they ask if state-level education course requirements for teacher certification, state-level test requirements for teacher certification, and the level of teachers' salaries relative to other college graduates' salaries in a state influence the probability that college graduates receive a degree in education.

They find that higher course work requirements or the presence of a certification examination reduces the probability that college graduates receive an education degree. Hence, careful consideration should be given to the usefulness of these tools in the process of attracting and selecting teachers. Contrary to the authors' expectations, teachers' relative salaries do not appear to influence the probability that students major in education. As Richard Murnane stressed at the conference, the use of statewide teacher salary data may not tell us much about the economic prospects that students face. What may be needed is more disaggregated data on relative earnings and job vacancies in smaller areas of each state.

Hanushek and Pace are careful to note, as did Murnane in his conference comments, that their analyses focus on only a fraction of the supply of teachers. They do not analyze delayed entry into the profession (people first entering more than six years after high school graduation), reentry of experienced teachers who had previously left teaching, or the determinants of exit from the profession. Previous research by Murnane and others suggests that teachers' salary levels are an important determinant of how long they stay in the profession.

David Monk and Jennifer King's paper focuses on high school mathematics and science teachers and their subject-matter competencies. More specifically, they are concerned with whether the number of courses that teachers completed in college in their subject-matter area influences how much their students learn. Previous research has suggested that the answer is yes, and this in turn suggests that subject-matter competency is one of the factors that should be important to school districts in framing hiring and compensation policies.

Monk and King ambitiously trace four possible routes via which teacher subject-matter competencies might be linked to teacher effectiveness. First, what a student's current teacher knows obviously may influence what the student learns in the class. Second, what the student's teacher in the previous academic year knew may influence not only the student's starting point for the current year, but also his or her attitude toward the subject and thus the amount that he or she learns in the current year. Third, what the student's teachers in still earlier years knew may similarly influence the student's learning trajectory in the current year. Finally, the competencies of all the teachers in the subject area in the school may influence student learning if these teachers share ideas or teaching materials, or if the less knowledgeable teachers can go to the more knowledgeable ones for advice.

Monk and King attempt to test which of these routes actually are important, using longitudinal data from a nationally representative sample of almost 3,000 high school students who were enrolled in the tenth grade in the fall of 1987. These data, which come from the Longitudinal Study of American Youth, contain information on the experience and subject-matter knowledge (courses taken) of each mathematics and science teacher in the school, on who each student's teachers were in each high school grade, and on each student's test scores in the two subjects in each grade. The data permit Monk and King to test whether the growth rates of a student's test scores over time are related to the subject-matter competencies of the student's current teacher in the subject, of the prior year teacher in the subject, of other prior teachers in the subject, or of all teachers in the school who teach the subject.

As Alan Krueger noted at the conference, the large proportion of variance in student test scores lying within, rather than across, the schools in these data makes it difficult to assess the importance of average school-level teacher characteristics on pupil performance. Even so, it would be premature to conclude that school-level faculty variability has little explanatory power.

The data are better suited for revealing the effects of prior teachers on students, and here there emerges some evidence of impact. The results are strongest when the prior teachers are looked at collectively; this implies that the cumulative effects of a sequence of high-quality teachers are noteworthy and warrant further study. However, the estimated impacts are never large in an absolute sense and tend to be inconsistent across different specifications of the underlying model.

The authors recognize that the number of courses teachers have taken in particular subject matters is not necessarily a good measure of the teachers' competencies in those subjects. What teachers actually know depends undoubtedly upon how well they performed in their course work, the difficulty of their courses, the quality of the instruction they received, and their own aptitude for mathematics and science. Unfortunately, Monk and King's data set contains none of these variables. Hence, the most one can prudently conclude from their paper is that there is reason to believe that teaching resources can influence pupil performance at multiple levels and that estimation of the relative magnitudes of the effects must await the collection of more refined measures of teachers' capabilities and inclinations.

The empirical results reported by Monk and King do not support strong policy initiatives such as placing much weight on the number of courses taken when hiring mathematics and science teachers or providing these teachers with salary increments for additional subject-matter courses taken. Rather, the study raises policymakers' sensitivities to the multiple means by which teaching resources can influence pupil performance.

The final two papers in the volume deal with the choices and the consequences of the decisions made by students approaching higher education. Despite the fact that nearly one-half of all first-time, first-year students attend a two-year or community college, few studies have examined how changes in tuition levels and college proximity influence students' decisions to attend two-year, as opposed to four-year, institutions. Community colleges have traditionally striven for equality of opportunity by charging low, or no, tuition. However, as noted above, the fiscal pressures faced by many states and localities in the early 1990s forced many community colleges to raise their tuition rates, sometimes faster than their four-year counterparts did.

Cecilia Rouse's paper is concerned with the implications of these policies. Did the traditionally low tuition levels and geographical convenience of community colleges attract students who otherwise would have attended four-year colleges? Or did community colleges instead provide educational opportunities for students who otherwise would not have attended any college? While the importance of this issue depends upon the extent to which the economic returns to education differ across institutional types and upon how a student's ultimate education level is influenced by the institution type in which he or she starts—issues that

Rouse herself has addressed in earlier work (Rouse 1993; Kane and Rouse 1993)—the questions she poses here are in need of answers.

Rouse uses data from two national surveys, the National Longitudinal Survey, Youth Cohort and High School and Beyond, to estimate multinomial logit models of the decisions of high school seniors to enroll in a two-year college, to enroll in a four-year college, or to not enroll in college at all in their first year after high school graduation. She finds that students who attend two-year colleges are much more likely to be the first in their families to attend college, are much less likely to have parents who graduated from four-year colleges, and are more likely to be of lower levels of measured ability than students who attend four-year colleges. Two-year colleges thus appear to provide a place in higher education for those not traditionally served by the four-year college system.

Crucially, Rouse also finds that two-year enrollment levels are much more sensitive to tuition levels than are four-year enrollment levels. Simulations she conducts suggest that the major effect of increasing tuition levels is to reduce enrollments at two-year colleges, which affects primarily students who otherwise would not attend college. In judging the desirability of raising tuitions at two-year colleges, these results must be kept in mind.

In her conference comments, Maria Hanratty suggested that focusing on high school seniors' decisions the year they graduate may overstate the long-run effects of higher tuition levels. Higher tuition levels may lead people to delay entry into two-year colleges as they work to build up assets to finance their education. While there are social and private gains to having people obtain their college education as early in their lives as possible, delayed entry into college is a less dire consequence of higher tuition levels than is no entry at all.

The final paper in the volume by Donna Rothstein and myself deals with another choice in higher education, that made by black students in the United States to attend either Historically Black Institutions (HBIs) or other institutions of higher education. The HBIs are the public and private institutions that were established to provide higher education for black students who were formally excluded from southern segregated white colleges and universities during much of our nation's history.

HBIs have become the subject of intense public policy debate in recent years for two reasons. First, court cases have been filed in a number of southern states that assert that black students continue to be underrepresented at traditionally white public institutions, that discriminatory admissions criteria are used by these institutions to exclude black students, and that per student funding levels, program availability, and library facilities are substantially poorer at the public HBIs than at other public institutions in these states. In 1992, the Supreme Court ruled that Mississippi had not done enough to eliminate racial segregation in its state-run higher educational institutions. Rather than mandating a remedy, however, the Court sent the case back to the lower courts for action.

What should the appropriate action be? Should it be to integrate more fully both the historically white and the historically black institutions by breaking down discriminatory admissions practices at the former and establishing some unique programs at the latter? Should effort be directed at equalizing per student expenditure levels and facilities between campuses, rather than at worrying about the racial distribution of students at each campus, even if such policies might result in "voluntary separate but equal" institutions? Or should HBIs be eliminated and their campuses either folded into the historically white institutions or abandoned altogether?

From an economic efficiency perspective, the appropriate policy response depends at least partially on whether HBIs provide unique advantages to black students that they cannot obtain at other institutions. To begin to address this issue, the first part of our paper uses data from the National Longitudinal Study of the High School Class of 1972 to ascertain whether black college students who attended HBIs in the early 1970s had higher graduation rates, improved early career labor market success, and higher probabilities of going on to graduate or professional schools than did their counterparts who attended other institutions.

We find that attendance at an HBI substantially enhances the probability that a black college student receives a bachelor's degree within seven years of starting college; however, on average, it has no apparent effects on the student's early career labor market success and on the probability of enrolling in graduate schooling. Thus, although black students in the 1970s uniquely benefitted educationally from attendance at an HBI, such attendance did not seem to yield an equal payoff in the labor market. Of course, as we note, and as conference discussant William Spriggs also noted, analysis of data from the 1970s does not necessarily provide a good guide for policy decisions in the 1990s. Consequently, in future research we will be updating these results using more recent data sets.

The second subject of policy debate relating to HBIs deals with the production and employment of black doctorates. Despite vigorous (or nonvigorous?) affirmative action efforts, the proportion of black faculty at major American universities is typically quite low. In part, this reflects the small number of black doctorates that are produced annually. Many people stress the need to increase the production of black doctorates to overcome this problem.

What is the best way to increase the flow of black students into doctoral programs? Should new doctoral programs be set up, or existing programs strengthened, at HBIs to enhance the flow of black doctorates? Or should attempts be made to recruit more black students from HBIs or from other institutions into existing doctoral programs at leading research universities? In part, the appropriate policy responses depend on the answer to another question: Do those black undergraduate students from HBIs who go on to doctoral study and those who get doctoral degrees at HBIs fare as well in the academic labor market as do their counterparts from other institutions?

To begin to answer these questions, the second part of our paper uses data from the 1987 to 1991 waves of the National Research Council's Survey of Earned Doctorates. Among the major findings is that black doctorates who receive their undergraduate degrees at HBIs are much less likely to receive their graduate degrees at a major research institution than are those black doctorates who attend a major research or selective liberal arts undergraduate institution. Similarly, among the black doctorates who enter academic careers, those with graduate degrees from HBIs are less likely to be employed in major American research or liberal arts institutions than are those who receive their graduate degrees from major research institutions.

An implication of these findings is that one way to increase the flow of black doctorates into faculty positions at major research universities and liberal arts colleges is to make sure that more students from HBIs attend graduate programs in major research universities. Faculty at some of the HBIs have stressed to us, however, that the goal of integrating the faculty at major northern universities is not one of their chief objectives. More important to them is increasing the total number of new black doctorates. None of the results presented in our paper directly bears on this objective, but methods to achieve it will be another subject of our future research.

The issues addressed in this volume are all important ones for educational policy. How can we assure an adequate flow of new teachers in general, and science and math teachers in particular, in the decade ahead? How can we maintain or increase the quality of our teachers? Should tuition levels at two-year public colleges be kept below those at four-year public colleges to guarantee access for students who otherwise would not attend college? What should public policy be toward Historically Black Institutions of higher education? How can we increase the number of black faculty members at major American colleges and universities? By both providing some answers to these questions and raising some new ones, this volume makes substantial contributions to the policy debate.

CHAPTER 1

Understanding Entry into the Teaching Profession

Eric A. Hanushek and Richard R. Pace

Remarkably little is known about who goes into teaching and why they go. This is particularly puzzling, given the interest that the subject of education has received for the past two decades. In recent experience, people have been concerned about the overall supply of qualified teachers, about the supply of teachers in various specialties such as math and science education, and about the quality of teachers attracted into the elementary and secondary schools. As a result of these concerns, many people seem willing to change radically the rules governing teaching jobs and the compensation for them on the belief (or hope) that a different group can be induced to enter teaching and that school performance will ultimately improve.

There are perennial projections of supply shortage. These projections reflect the recent declines in the production of new teachers (NCES 1992), the clear upturn in the student population occurring now, and the anticipation of high retirement rates of teachers over the next decade. Many have questioned if aggregate shortages will, in fact, materialize, in part because of the large "reserve army" of potential teachers who could return to teaching. This questioning has led to a different set of issues—whether or not there will be a shortage of high-quality teachers and whether or not there will be sufficient numbers of particular subject-matter teachers, such as math and science teachers. Without getting into questions about the sort of shortages that may materialize, it is clear that large questions remain about who is being prepared for teaching and what these people respond to in making career decisions.

The dearth of existing analysis allows many statements to be simply repeated and used in the development of policies, whether or not

We would like to thank Stanley Engerman, Richard Murnane, Orley Ashenfelter, and Robert Strauss for their helpful comments.

these statements are accurate or relevant. For example, much of the information we have about the characteristics and quality of teachers does not come from information about teachers per se but, instead, comes from employing such information as SAT performance and other characteristics of high school seniors who indicate that they plan to become teachers.[1] The group of aspirants is not, however, the group that eventually enters the teaching profession. Considerable shuffling takes place, as many who originally expressed interest leave the study of teaching, only to be replaced by a new group that had not previously thought of teaching.

BACKGROUND AND DATA

Analysis of the supply of teachers is quite complicated because individuals enter teaching jobs from various places (Murnane et al. 1991; Boe and Guilford 1992; Strauss 1993). At any point in time, the pool of newly hired teachers includes a mixture of recent college graduates, of returning teachers who had been out of the profession for some time, and of past college graduates who have either been retrained or are currently entering teaching for the first time.

The focus of this paper is the decision all of these people make to prepare for elementary and secondary teaching. We presume that this is the key step in setting potential teacher supply because late entrants and reentrants still went through the phase of teacher preparation. We also consider whether or not first jobs involve teaching, but the limited time span of the study we use here inhibits making very broad generalizations from this.

Most information about decisions that determine the occupational choices of teachers involve analyzing either aspirations data—collected long before preparation for teaching or job choices are completed—or data on the current stock of teachers. These data, which provide insights into some issues, do not permit attention to the key points in the decision process or to how fundamental factors such as certification requirements and the like influence teacher preparation and supply.

We view the process of entry into the teaching profession as a series of sequential decisions. The process begins with the development of career goals and the initial aspirations of students in high school. We trace how the group that initially aspires to teach wends its way through the educational system and, specifically, which of these students actually emerge fully prepared to teach. The process also involves the infusion of new people who turn to teaching even though they did not have early aspirations to do so. We consider how these people compare with those who "always" wanted to teach.

This analysis employs the longitudinal data from the High School and Beyond (HSB) survey to follow students from high school through college. The first wave of the HSB data was collected from a group of high school seniors in 1980; these students were subsequently followed through 1986.[2]

The HSB data have a number of strengths for our study. First, the survey's longitudinal design permits direct investigation of the choices students are making at each stage of their education. Thus, it is possible to follow individual students from high school through college, observing at each stage whether or not a student is preparing for a teaching career. Second, its large national sample provides information on how varying certification requirements and rewards for teachers affect students' choices. Third, since all students were given standardized achievement tests, there is a rough measure of "quality" that can be introduced.

The HSB data are not, however, without weaknesses. The survey tracks a single cohort through school and therefore limits the generalizations that can be made about other times and cohorts. Additionally, the data provide just initial choices and actions. The seniors in 1980, at best, graduated from college in 1984, but common patterns of delayed completion of college show that many of the sampled students did not graduate by then. This makes it particularly difficult to observe employment decisions of potential teachers before the end of the study. Movement into and out of teaching over extended periods of time by many in the profession (Murnane et al. 1991) also severely limits making generalizations past those that derive from training decisions.

An important part of this analysis is the quality of individuals choosing teaching. This investigation cannot, however, observe actual teaching performance of any individuals, so the measurement of quality must rely on surrogates for future performance. The primary measure of quality of potential teachers employs the composite test score from the HSB battery of achievement tests given in 1980. This composite score combines the results of reading, vocabulary, and mathematics exams.

Our primary aim is to study the supply of high-quality teachers, but we do not have an opportunity to observe directly the quality of classroom instruction by any of the sampled individuals. Indeed, nobody has ever been able to do that in a systematic way. It is plausible, however, to believe that "smarter" teachers with higher levels of achievement could perform better in the classroom. This logic also motivates one of the few existing studies of teacher supply that considers differences in quality (Manski 1987). Separate studies of educational production functions have tended to find some positive relationship between measured teacher achievement and student performance, although this finding is far from universal.[3]

The analysis here first provides a descriptive overview of the path to teaching careers. It then turns to an investigation of whether or not the differences in requirements and rewards across states influence these observed patterns.

OVERALL TRANSITION PATTERNS

This section identifies the movement of students into and out of training programs for elementary and secondary teaching. Special attention is given to students who aspire to elementary and secondary teaching during their senior year in high school, and they are followed through college. This group has a continually stronger attachment to the possibility of teaching than do high school students or college entrants as a whole.

A point of concentration is the top of the achievement distribution. The comparison employed traces students who scored in the top quarter of the test distribution of those who attended a regular, academic, postsecondary program during the first two years after high school graduation.

This analysis is a snapshot that views the progression of one cohort through its postsecondary studies. As such, it cannot distinguish between time-specific factors and the normal transition and aging process. The subsequent investigation of variations in transition probabilities across different states, however, provides some indication of more fundamental driving forces.

We begin with the entire sample of high school seniors in 1980 and trace their path through college and through teaching preparation. Table 1.1 is divided into two parallel views of teachers engaged in preparation for teaching and, ultimately, employed in a teaching occupation by spring 1986. The left half of the table ("Original aspirants") takes a fixed group of students—those high school students who aspired to a teaching job in elementary and secondary schools in their senior year—and follows their actual choices. The right half of the table ("In teaching at each point") provides a complete snapshot of all those engaged in the specified teacher preparation at each point, combining the original aspirants with the new

Table 1.1. Teacher Preparation Transitions by Ability and Aspirations: Entire Sample

Status (Year)	Original Aspirants			In Teaching at Each Point			
	% Top Half	% Top Quartile	N	% Orig. Aspirants	% Top Half	% Top Quartile	N
Aspire to teach senior year HS (1980)	40.2	17.4	352	100	40.2	17.4	352
In teacher training (1982)	45.5	21.6	130	41.6	40.0	15.5	362
In teacher training (1984)	45.1	16.8	93	36.4	51.7	21.6	296
Graduated college, teacher prepared (1986)	50.0	21.5	56	41.4	48.4	21.1	154
Actively teaching (1986)	51.5	33.1	64	34.1	59.2	28.4	223

Note: Ability distribution is based on reading, vocabulary, and mathematics test scores of the sample of students who had ever been enrolled in an academic postsecondary program by the time of the first HSB follow-up.

entrants into teacher preparation. We employ weighted data since we are interested in tracking the population over time.

There are some simple lessons that we take away from this overview.

1. Only a small proportion of high school students who aspire to teach ever complete a bachelor's degree with a specialty in teaching and education. Following the group of original aspirants, we find that only 22.2 percent graduated by 1986 having completed a teacher preparation program.[4] Moreover, of the total students who graduated from teacher training, only about two-fifths (41.4 percent) thought they would be teachers when they were in high school.[5] This is very important because it suggests that simply looking at statistics of aspirants does not characterize very well who actually prepares for teaching. A higher number of people than those completing teacher preparation were actually teaching in elementary and secondary schools in 1986,[6] and the representation of original aspirants in the actual teachers was even lower.

2. There is a significant influx of people at each stage, but, not surprisingly, the biggest transition comes between the senior year of high school and the sophomore year of college. Thus, as early as two years following graduation, less than half of those who originally aspired to

teaching were enrolled in actual teacher preparation programs at the college level. This seems straightforward: Most people do not settle on an academic program until after having attended college for some time.

3. Individuals who aspire to be teachers in high school are below average in high school achievement. Only 40.2 percent of aspirants ranked in the top half of the achievement distribution, which is defined by the test scores of all students who attended college by 1982 (two years after graduation from high school). There are, more importantly, noticeably fewer aspirants in the very top of the distribution, although there is significant representation in the top. About 17 percent of the aspirants are found in the top quartile of the achievement distribution.

4. A disproportionate number of original aspirants who will eventually turn to other occupations come from the bottom portion of the distribution.[7] Thus, those who remain are more heavily weighted in the right half of the distribution. The pattern over time is very interesting nevertheless. Those studying education in the 1982 survey at roughly the spring of their sophomore year look similar in the aggregate to the whole pool of original aspirants in terms of being from the lower half of the distribution. By 1986, however, half of students who maintained teaching goals and graduated from a teacher preparation program came from the top half of the achievement distribution of all entering college students, and over 20 percent came from the top quartile of entering students. Moreover, of those aspirants who were actually teaching in elementary and secondary schools by the time of the final survey (1986), a full third came from the top quartile of the initial distribution. Thus, although some relatively low achievers study education, graduation and actual employment apparently represent for them hurdles too large to overcome; the group that succeeds, therefore, does not appear to be comprised of the "dregs," as some have suggested.

5. The injections into the system, unlike the distribution of original aspirants, tend to be relatively high-ability students (above the median, although not necessarily in the top quartile). The exception is the data from 1982, where those who moved into teaching were weighted toward the bottom portion of the distribution. By the time of graduation and of acceptance of a teaching job, the people who switched into teaching during their college years look quite similar in distribution to those remaining students who always wanted to teach.

6. Those obtaining a teacher's degree have higher ability than all original aspirants. Many who sought teaching degrees had not received a B.A. degree by spring of the sixth year after high school graduation. Of the original aspirants, only 66.2 percent who were studying education in

1984 had graduated by 1986; similarly, about half of all people who were studying education in 1984 had completed their degree requirements by spring 1986. Those not receiving a degree, not surprisingly, tended to come from the lower half of the overall distribution. Thus, in terms of the shape of the distribution of graduates with teaching degrees, it is stronger than that of the original aspirants and, indeed, very close to a representative draw from the overall distribution of college attenders. (However, it may be that the available HSB follow-ups concluded too early to capture the full distribution of graduates. Indeed, the low achievers may eventually complete training, which would imply that the distribution of those prepared to teach is lower than that of the graduates found in spring 1986.)

7. The measured ability of all college graduates is, however, higher than that of graduates completing teacher training. Of all college graduates (by 1986 in the HSB data set), 67 percent ranked in the top half of the achievement distribution of college entrants, and 42 percent came from the top quartile. The graduates with teaching credentials come close to replicating the initial distribution of college students but fall down noticeably in the distribution of all college graduates.

8. The picture of teacher preparation varies sharply by gender. Tables 1.2 and 1.3 display the breakdown of transitions for males and females, respectively. A number of generalizations are apparent. First, and quite obviously, males represent only a small part of the sample—less than 20 percent of potential and actual teachers. Second, males that are committed to teaching rank higher than females in the achievement distribution at almost every observation point. This holds for the original aspirants and the new injections into teaching. Third, women are much more likely than men to stay in teaching once they express an interest in high school (even though the absolute continuation rates are low even for women, with about 20 percent entering teaching by 1986). The picture that emerges is one in which teaching remains a "standard" occupation for women in ways that it is not for men, and in which men who graduate and enter teaching tend to be from the higher achievement groups.

9. The movements in and out of teacher training by gender tend to follow quite different patterns. For males, injections into training are generally lower in ability than are original aspirants. For females, the opposite is true: The new entrants into teacher training tend to be of higher ability than those who originally planned on a teaching career and who stay with it through graduation. Thus, looking at only people who

Table 1.2. Teacher Preparation Transitions by Ability and Aspirations: Males

Status (Year)	Original Aspirants			In Teaching at Each Point			
	% Top Half	% Top Quartile	N	% Orig. Aspirants	% Top Half	% Top Quartile	N
Aspire to teach senior year HS (1980)	53.3	22.3	64	100	53.3	22.3	64
In teacher training (1982)	61.7	33.7	12	22.7	46.4	16.2	71
In teacher training (1984)	69.8	34.0	13	18.1	50.7	22.4	75
Graduated college, teacher prepared (1986)	60.2	40.0	8	30.2	44.5	23.9	28
Actively teaching (1986)	60.2	45.5	8	23.1	62.5	31.1	43

Note: Ability distribution is based on reading, vocabulary, and mathematics test scores of the sample of students who had ever been enrolled in an academic postsecondary program by the time of the first HSB follow-up.

aspire to teach while in high school leads to downward biases in quality for females and upward biases for males.

10. The pattern also differs sharply by race. Tables 1.4, 1.5, and 1.6 present the patterns for blacks, Hispanics, and whites. While the samples for minority groups are small, high-quality (top half or top quartile) blacks exit from teaching throughout the educational process, and they are not replaced with high-quality injections. What is more, a much smaller proportion of eligible blacks than whites will stay with teaching careers. Again, although the samples get quite small, Hispanics are more likely than blacks to enter and to stay in teacher training programs. And those Hispanics who do enter teaching tend to be noticeably higher in the achievement distribution than the remaining blacks.

FACTORS INFLUENCING TEACHER PREPARATION AND ENTRY

The previous descriptions of the flows into and out of a teacher preparation program and the completions of training give a coarse overview of entry into teaching. Nevertheless, they obscure what could

Table 1.3. Teacher Preparation Transitions by Ability and Aspirations: Females

Status (Year)	Original Aspirants			In Teaching at Each Point			
	% Top Half	% Top Quartile	N	% Orig. Aspirants	% Top Half	% Top Quartile	N
Aspire to teach senior year HS (1980)	37.7	16.4	288	100	37.7	16.4	288
In teacher training (1982)	44.0	20.5	118	44.9	39.0	15.3	291
In teacher training (1984)	41.7	14.4	80	42.3	52.1	21.3	221
Graduated college, teacher prepared (1986)	48.3	18.5	48	44.1	49.3	20.5	126
Actively teaching (1986)	50.2	31.3	56	36.5	58.5	27.7	180

Note: Ability distribution is based on reading, vocabulary, and mathematics test scores of the sample of students who had ever been enrolled in an academic postsecondary program by the time of the first HSB follow-up.

be important differences based upon the detailed circumstances facing individual students. While these data do not permit looking at individual-specific demand considerations, they do permit looking at variations across states, and this provides an opportunity to look at some of the most debated issues of educational policy.

Individual states employ quite distinct policies with respect to certification requirements, work conditions and rules, and compensation. And, indeed, many reform proposals begin with the notion of working through state-level policies. One set of policies would improve the compensation and conditions of employment for teachers and would work to expand the pool of potential teachers. A further set of policies would tighten the requirements for teaching, through such things as extended training requirements, testing programs, and the like.

The approach here is to combine the High School and Beyond data with information about the structure of teaching requirements and pay for teachers.[8] We then attempt to explain variations in the probability of preparing for teaching careers by variations in state requirements and state economic conditions, in addition to the background factors considered previously.

Table 1.4. Teacher Preparation Transitions by Ability and Aspirations: Blacks

Status (Year)	Original Aspirants			In Teaching at Each Point			
	% Top Half	% Top Quartile	N	% Orig. Aspirants	% Top Half	% Top Quartile	N
Aspire to teach senior year HS (1980)	17.3	7.5	66	100	17.3	7.5	66
In teacher training (1982)	24.1	0.0	13	37.4	9.3	0.0	56
In teacher training (1984)	0.0	0.0	7	18.1	8.7	0.2	44
Graduated college, teacher prepared (1986)	0.0	0.0	5	36.5	0.0	0.0	18
Actively teaching (1986)	0.0	0.0	5	23.4	2.7	0.2	30

Note: Ability distribution is based on reading, vocabulary, and mathematics test scores of the sample of students who had ever been enrolled in an academic postsecondary program by the time of the first HSB follow-up.

We concentrate on the probability that an individual has graduated with an education degree, given that the student graduated from college by 1986. As noted above, obtaining a teaching degree is not the only route into teaching, but it is by far the most common.

Our modeling work concentrates on three factors that have been featured in current discussions of teacher supply policies: the amount of teacher-specific course work that is required for certification; the use of teacher tests for certification; and the relative earnings of teachers. These matters, which are some of the most important policies controlled at the state level, have been highlighted for change—even though the recommended changes have not always pointed in the same direction.

Policy recommendations about course-work requirements have actually gone in all directions. Considerable tension exists. States periodically review their requirements and frequently call for the introduction of new and additional course requirements for teacher preparation. Conversely, another set of arguments suggests that these undergraduate course-work requirements should be lowered significantly, if not dropped. The lowering of undergraduate requirements has been argued as appropriate

Table 1.5. *Teacher Preparation Transitions by Ability and Aspirations: Hispanics*

Status (Year)	Original Aspirants			In Teaching at Each Point			
	% Top Half	% Top Quartile	N	% Orig. Aspirants	% Top Half	% Top Quartile	N
Aspire to teach senior year HS (1980)	6.5	4.6	83	100	6.5	4.6	83
In teacher training (1982)	10.2	9.8	30	41.1	11.5	4.6	87
In teacher training (1984)	13.5	12.3	17	25.5	15.6	6.6	57
Graduated college, teacher prepared (1986)	2.1	2.1	7	18.2	12.8	0.4	29
Actively teaching (1986)	33.4	30.5	9	13.3	23.1	12.1	44

Note: Ability distribution is based on reading, vocabulary, and mathematics test scores of the sample of students who had ever been enrolled in an academic postsecondary program by the time of the first HSB follow-up.

Table 1.6. *Teacher Preparation Transitions by Ability and Aspirations: Whites*

Status (Year)	Original Aspirants			In Teaching at Each Point			
	% Top Half	% Top Quartile	N	% Orig. Aspirants	% Top Half	% Top Quartile	N
Aspire to teach senior year HS (1980)	46.2	20.0	190	100	46.2	20.0	190
In teacher training (1982)	50.4	24.7	85	42.6	45.7	18.1	207
In teacher training (1984)	48.0	17.6	68	38.4	57.1	24.1	191
Graduated college, teacher prepared (1986)	53.2	22.7	43	43.2	52.5	23.4	105
Actively teaching (1986)	54.3	34.6	48	36.9	65.4	32.1	137

Note: Ability distribution is based on reading, vocabulary, and mathematics test scores of the sample of students who had ever been enrolled in an academic postsecondary program by the time of the first HSB follow-up.

because such requirements for education courses crowd out other undergraduate courses that are hypothesized to be more important. Some suggest that it is better to develop the thorough subject-matter knowledge and analytical ability that is central to liberal arts preparation; others concentrate on the potentially adverse supply effects that result from a person having to commit fully to a teaching career while cutting off other career possibilities. Those advocating loosening the requirements for undergraduate preparation split, however, on where to take these recommendations. Some feel that relaxing or eliminating the undergraduate requirements should go hand in hand with a new requirement of master's-level training in education (cf. Carnegie Forum 1986 and Holmes Group 1986). Others believe that alternative strategies, such as New Jersey's Provisional Teacher Program, offer much more hope (Murnane et al. 1991). Again, while this work cannot assess the outcomes of teacher training requirements in terms of student learning,[9] it can look at the effects of different requirements on the supply of trained teachers.

The testing of teachers is another controversial area. Since 1980, a majority of states has enacted legislation requiring teachers to take and pass a test before initial certification (see Strauss 1994 for a discussion of potential policies). The most common test is the National Teacher Examination (NTE), but a number of states have developed alternatives. A variety of questions has been raised about this. Are teacher test performance and teaching performance highly correlated? Are the tests discriminatory? Do the tests erect an artificial barrier to entry into teaching? We look at whether the use of such tests influences student decisions on teacher preparation.

Finally, the most frequently suggested policy for improving the quality of the teaching force is to increase the compensation of teachers. The relative salaries of teachers, displayed in Table 1.7, fell noticeably after World War II. The pattern is, however, a bit different than conventional wisdom typically suggests since the sharpest decline came before 1960 for men but only recently for women. The policy argument remains, nonetheless, straightforward: Higher salaries will attract a larger and more qualified pool of applicants. It is possible to test this hypothesis by observing variations in the relative earnings of teachers compared to those in other occupations.

The statistical analysis considers how these various factors affect the probability of completing a teacher training program. The variable definitions, along with descriptive statistics, are found in Table 1.8 and probit estimates of student decisions for teacher training appear in Table 1.9. Overall by 1986, 12.5 percent of the college graduates were prepared for

Table 1.7. *Average Earnings of Teachers as a Proportion of Earnings of Nonteaching College Graduates*

Year	Men	Women
1940	0.75	1.01
1950	0.67	0.99
1960	0.69	0.96
1970	0.70	0.91
1980	0.67	0.88
1990	0.65	0.80

Source: U.S. Bureau of the Census, *Census of Population and Housing,* 1940, 1950, 1960, 1970, 1980, 1990.
Note: Average earnings of nonteachers is a weighted average of earnings based on the sex and age composition of teachers.

Table 1.8. *Descriptive Statistics for Teacher Preparation Models (N = 1,325)*

Variable	Mean	Definition
Male	.438 (.496)	= 1 if male; = 0 if female
Hispanic	.155 (.362)	= 1 if Hispanic or Spanish; = 0 otherwise
Native American	.005 (.073)	= 1 if Native American or Alaskan; = 0 otherwise
Asian	.048 (.214)	= 1 if Asian or Pacific Islander; = 0 otherwise
Black	.152 (.359)	= 1 if African-American; = 0 otherwise
Base test score	55.96 (7.44)	Student combined mathematics, reading, and vocabulary test score, base year (1980)
TEST	.435 (.496)	= 1 if state requires testing for initial certification; = 0 otherwise[a]
PROFCRDT	18.91 (11.47)	Number of professional education credits required by state for certification[b]
RELEARN	1.011 (.095)	Mean starting teacher salary from 1980 HSB survey relative to mean 1980 census annual earnings of all females age 25–34 with 4 years of college, by state

Note: Figures in parentheses represent standard deviations.
[a] *Source:* Goertz, Ekstrom, and Coley (1984).
[b] *Source:* Woellner (1982).

Table 1.9. Probit Estimates of Probability of Earning Bachelor's Degree in Education (Conditional upon Receiving Bachelor's Degree)

Variable	(1)	(2)	(3)	(4)
Male	−0.645***	−0.646***	−0.646***	−0.647***
	(0.11)	(0.11)	(0.11)	(0.11)
Hispanic	−0.242*	−0.222	−0.260*	−0.238
	(0.15)	(0.15)	(0.15)	(0.15)
Native American	−0.105	−0.111	−0.133	−0.143
	(0.58)	(0.58)	(0.58)	(0.58)
Asian	−1.176***	−1.169***	−1.19***	−1.18***
	(0.44)	(0.44)	(0.44)	(0.44)
Black	−0.596***	−0.587***	−0.404**	−0.376*
	(0.16)	(0.16)	(0.20)	(0.21)
Base test score	−0.048***	−0.048***	−0.049***	−0.049***
	(0.01)	(0.01)	(0.01)	(0.01)
TEST	−0.258**	−0.245**	−0.195*	−0.173
	(0.11)	(0.11)	(0.11)	(0.12)
PROFCRDT	−0.008*	−0.008*	−0.008*	−0.008*
	(0.004)	(0.004)	(0.004)	(0.004)
RELEARN		0.377		0.487
		(0.52)		(0.52)
Black × TEST			−0.435	−0.472
			(0.30)	(0.30)
Intercept	2.040***	1.625**	2.062***	1.528**
	(0.44)	(0.72)	(0.44)	(0.72)

Note: Column headings are as follows: (1) Effects of the number of professional credits in undergraduate training required and of the use of either the NTE test or a state test for certification; (2) Relative earnings of teachers in each state; (3) and (4) Interactions between student race and test requirements. Figures in parentheses represent standard errors.

*p < .10   **p < .05   ***p < .01

teaching careers. The probit estimates in Table 1.9 indicate the marginal effects of each factor. The separate columns vary in the characterization of state factors. The first column considers just the effects of the number of professional credits in undergraduate training required and of the use of either the NTE test or a state test for certification; the second column adds the relative earnings of teachers in each state; and the third and fourth allow for interactions between student race and test requirements. In general, the estimates are very stable across specifications, so we will simply report the results from column 2 unless otherwise indicated.

The top portion of Table 1.9 provides a multivariate extension of the previous descriptive analyses of student choices. Quite clearly, those preparing for teaching are heavily concentrated among white females. At the sample means, the white male preparation rate is 10 percentage points lower. Similarly, Asians (18.2 percentage points) and blacks (9.2 percentage points) are more likely to train in fields other than teaching.

Holding constant race and gender, people scoring higher on the base-year test are less likely to enter teaching. A move from the mean to one standard deviation above the mean on the base-year test score implies a 5.5 percentage point decline in the probability of training for teaching.

The bottom portion of the table is concerned with the direct state policy instruments discussed. The requirements for professional credits (PROFCRDT) vary quite widely across states, with an average of nineteen credits and a standard deviation of over eleven credits. An increased requirement lowers the probability of completing a teacher's preparation curriculum, with an added ten credits reducing teaching preparation by 1.2 percentage points.

The use of tests for certification (TEST) also reduces the probability of teacher training. Other things being equal, teacher preparation will be 4 percentage points lower in a state requiring either the NTE or another statewide test. This measure is clearly quite crude because it does not provide an indication of differential difficulty in passing tests.[10] Nonetheless, these requirements have strong effects on teacher preparation, leading to a 32 percent average reduction in the rate of teacher preparation. Murnane et al. (1991) suggest that the use of certification tests may have differential effects on minorities, particularly blacks. To analyze this, the last two columns of Table 1.9 include an interaction between whether or not the student is black and the use of a certification test. While these estimates indicate a negative interaction—that is, black students react more strongly to the use of tests than do other students—the estimated effects are statistically insignificant.

Finally, the models also consider the effect of relative teacher earnings. This measure (RELEARN) compares HSB data on entry salaries for teachers with average earnings of female college graduates, aged twenty-five to thirty-four, in each state. While the point estimates indicate that higher relative earnings elicit a positive supply response, the magnitude is extraordinarily small, and the effects are not significantly different from zero. These negligible earnings effects could be explained by measurement difficulties. The earnings measures differ only by state and refer only to 1980. Thus, if individuals have different expectations based either on more local information or on their forecasts of the future, these estimates could be biased downward. Nevertheless, they suggest that overall salary actions will not have a large short run effect on training and supply.

Because of the special concern about high-ability students and their choices, the preceding analysis was duplicated for students in the top quartile of those attending college. Of the 499 students in the top quartile who graduated from college by 1986, 6.2 percent completed teacher training (as compared to 12.5 percent for the entire population of graduates). Interestingly, however, the estimated probit models of choice for the top quartile are not significantly different from those for the rest of the population.

In the course of the investigation, several other characteristics of state programs were examined. The TEST variable was disaggregated into the NTE and other state-specified tests; variables for the use of forgivable loans for students in education programs and for a certification requirement of obtaining a master's degree were introduced; and the measure of course requirements was expanded to include requirements past professional education credits. None of these proved significant in the analyses. This, however, may simply reflect the crudeness of the measures and the limited variation in these requirements across the states.

INTERPRETATION AND CONCLUSIONS

This study stops considerably short of uncovering what we would like to know about teacher supply. It finds a number of factors that affect teacher preparation and thus teacher supply. It cannot, however, easily carry this through to statements about ultimate impacts on student learning.

The descriptive analysis and the subsequent models of student choice underscore what has been known for some time. White females are much more likely to complete teacher preparation than are males or members of racial and ethnic minority groups. Moreover, lower ability students, as measured by cognitive achievement tests, are more likely than higher ability students to enter teaching.

The most significant findings, however, relate to state requirements. The barriers that states set up for certification indeed inhibit supply. The prospect of taking an examination for certification lowers the rate of teacher preparation, everything else equal. Likewise, increased course requirements for professional education depress supply. Nothing, of course, is said here about whether or not these requirements are appropriate (although some have argued that they are not). These results merely indicate that such requirements are costly in terms of a smaller pool of trained teachers.

The results for the effects of teacher salaries do not indicate that this is a particularly powerful influence on student choices. Even though relative earnings of teachers compared to all college graduates vary considerably across the nation, they do not have a large or statistically significant impact on student preparation for teaching.

The preliminary glimpse at actual entry into the teaching profession shows similar patterns across states. The use of teacher examinations for certification purposes has the clearest impact on lessening supply. Nonetheless, the data on actual teaching come too early in potential careers to give a complete picture of what supply ultimately will look like.

What is needed is to merge information about actual teaching ability with information about factors affecting supply. Such an objective is obviously much more easily stated than accomplished. All of the analytical work on schools and educational performance suggests that the simple, commonly measured attributes of teachers, such as degree level or amount of teaching experience, are not closely related to the classroom performance of the teacher. Given this, direct estimation of supply functions for teachers is very difficult.

The quality measure of this study—cognitive test performance of students prior to college entry—has two problems. While past work suggests teacher test performance is somewhat related to student performance, the relationship is far from perfect. Additionally, these are tests taken prior to attending college, thus they ignore any differential value added by college experiences.

All of these arguments suggest that the study of teacher supply must be more directly related to actual classroom performance. The research design that accomplishes this is quite complicated. Moreover, the only direct method may involve some degree of experimentation. But even that entails difficulties if one wishes to trace the full response of student decisions.

Multilevel Teacher Resource Effects on Pupil Performance in Secondary Mathematics and Science: The Case of Teacher Subject-Matter Preparation

David H. Monk and Jennifer A. King

It is well established that schools exert influence on pupil performance at multiple organizational levels. There are, for example, classroom effects that derive from the characteristics and activities of a student's teacher and fellow students within a given class. In addition, there are school-level effects that can take various forms. Disruptive incidents, for example, need not occur within a student's classroom to have impact on pupil performance (Summers and Wolfe 1977). Similarly, research has shown that the degree to which a school functions as a supportive community can have bearing on students' learning gains (Bryk and Driscoll 1988), and it is clear that such phenomena transcend the characteristics of individual classrooms (Rowan, Raudenbush, and Kang 1991).

Analogous effects can be discerned at either more or less centralized levels of decision making within schools. For example, groups are often formed within classes, and research has dealt with the effects of group attributes on the learning of students within, as well as across, groups (Barr and Dreeben 1983; Dreeben and Barr 1988; Gamoran 1987; Hallinan and Sorensen 1985). Local education agencies or districts frequently consist of numerous discrete schools, and it is possible to conceive of district attributes that are logically related to pupil performance (Bidwell

The paper has been prepared for the second annual Cornell-Princeton policy conference. It is part of the research program of the Finance Center of the Consortium for Policy Research in Education (CPRE), a consortium of the University of Southern California, Rutgers University, Cornell University, Harvard University, Michigan State University, Stanford University and the University of Wisconsin-Madison. The work was supported by grant number R1178G10039 from the U.S. Department of Education, Office of Educational Research and Improvement. The views expressed are those of the authors and are not necessarily shared by USC, CPRE or its partners, or the U.S. Department of Education. We would like to thank Dominic Brewer, Ronald Ehrenberg, Ronald Ferguson, Emil Haller, and Alan Krueger for their insightful comments on earlier drafts of this paper.

and Kasarda 1975). A good example of such a district-level attribute is policy regarding within-district teacher transfers.

In this study, we use a multilevel approach to explore the effects of teachers' subject-matter preparation on the performance gains of their pupils. We have chosen to examine teacher preparation from a multilevel perspective for three reasons. First, there is evidence that measures of what teachers know and can do have independent effects on pupil performance gains in school settings. This appears to be a promising line of research that is generating insight into the ingredients of good schooling. Our presumption is that the extent of subject-specific training in a teacher's background has bearing on what that teacher knows and can do in a classroom.

Second, there are reasons for thinking that the effects of teacher subject-matter preparation are likely to exist at multiple levels of schooling organizations. Individual teachers interact in numerous ways with their colleagues, and students can experience many different teachers over time. These phenomena can be expected to generate both school- and classroom-level effects.

Finally, our inquiry is relevant to policymaking, given the growing interest in linking teacher compensation programs with measures of what teachers know and can accomplish (Odden and Conley 1991). While some are skeptical about the wisdom of such high-stakes accountability systems for teachers (see, for example, Millman and Sykes 1992), it is important to know more about the kind of gains that can be realized from various types of teacher preparation.

In the next section, we explain the multilevel conceptualization of teacher resources that undergirds the study. We also further develop our rationale for focusing attention on the subject-matter preparation of teachers. The third section provides a description of our data and methods, and the fourth reports our findings. The chapter concludes by discussing our findings and considering implications for policy.

CONCEPTUAL ISSUES

Our primary task is to explore the distinction between students' proximate and more distant teachers and to think through the influence each type of instructional resource is likely to have on pupil performance.

DISTINGUISHING AMONG DIFFERENT LEVELS OF TEACHING RESOURCES

We begin by defining a student's proximate teacher to be an individual teacher who has primary responsibility for a given student's instruction in a particular area of the curriculum at a given point in time.[1] By defining the proximate teacher in this way, we indirectly define a broad and unwieldy class or set of "nonproximate" teachers.

We can set bounds on this unwieldy set by focusing attention on just those teaching resources present within a given organizational structure, say, a school. And we can restrict the set further by distinguishing among teaching specialties.[2] For our purposes here, it is useful to impose these restrictions, and from this point forward we shall use the term "nonproximate" to refer to subject-specific teaching resources (e.g., mathematics or English) that are present within a given student's school.

We are interested in contrasting the effects of proximate teachers to the effects of these nonproximate teachers on pupils' performance gains. Although there are reasons for expecting effects from both types of teaching resources, our central thesis is that the directness of the contact enjoyed by the proximate teacher will translate into relatively large effects on pupil performance.

We can gain additional insight into the implications of our thesis by recognizing that nonproximate teachers themselves vary in terms of the directness of contact with students. It is possible to identify three conceptually distinct, but overlapping, levels of contact that are relatively easy to order in terms of their directness: (1) the immediate past teacher in a given subject area; (2) the set of previous teachers a student has had in a given subject area over some specified period of time; and (3) the set of all teachers in a school who teach courses in a given subject area.

The immediate past teacher is an individual teacher and is comparable in this respect to the proximate teacher. Each can be described in terms of selected individual attributes. In contrast, the sets of previous teachers and all subject-matter specialists within the school will almost always involve several teachers. These sets can be characterized using summary statistics such as the average or level of variation in selected attributes of the sets' members. In addition, information about time can be used to characterize these sets in terms of how the members are ordered.

CONCEPTUALIZING THE EFFECTS OF TEACHING RESOURCES AT DIFFERENT LEVELS

Proximate Teacher. Of all the teaching resources we are considering, the proximate teacher has the most direct, and presumably most important, impact on the performance gains of students. The proximate teacher has discretion over how much time he or she devotes to both the student in question and the larger class.[3] The proximate teacher also has some discretion over the quality of the teaching resource that is provided.[4] In addition to the quantity and quality of teaching resources being provided, the proximate teacher exercises some discretion over the supply of other types of instructional resources (e.g., the time and effort of teacher aides, materials, supplies, computer-assisted instruction, and so on).

Immediate Past Teacher. The performance of a student during period t can be influenced by the student's teacher during period $t-1$ in several different ways. These effects can be categorized as either productivity effects or supply effects, and we discuss each in turn. In addition, we discuss an interesting combination of productivity and supply effects.

Productivity effects. A previous teacher can influence a student's subsequent ability to benefit from whatever future instructional resources, both teaching and nonteaching, that might be forthcoming. For example, a previous teacher may have somehow developed the student into a more fertile receiver of whatever future resources are supplied, and this can be construed as a gain in the marginal productivities of these future resources. Such a result suggests that an investment in human capital took place in the form of the work of the previous teacher. The student gains an asset that in principle can pay dividends over a potentially lengthy period of time. A reversed kind of disinvestment may also be possible. Having a "bad" teacher one year can lower the marginal productivities of subsequently provided resources.

Supply effects. The work of a previous teacher can also influence the quantity of resources (both teaching and nonteaching) that is subsequently supplied to a student. This is another argument involving human capital. It suggests that the previous teacher builds an asset that generates benefits by "attracting" an enhanced supply of future instructional resources.

Perhaps the most important supply effect stems from the influence a previous teacher can have on students' own willingness to supply time and effort to their studies. A previous teacher can instill a love for a subject in particular or for learning in general that lasts long after the direct contact with the teacher ceases.

Moreover, it may be through a previous teacher's effect on students' willingness to supply their own time and effort to learning activities that the previous teacher can have an effect on the future supply of teacher and other schooling resources. The willingness of students to devote extra time and effort to their studies may well account for what makes the student "attractive" for subsequent teachers.

A reversed result is also possible. If a previous teacher extinguishes a student's interest in a subject and the student responds by withdrawing time and effort from the subsequent study, there may be a response in kind on the part of subsequent teachers.

Combination effects. There is an additional means by which a previous teacher can affect current pupil performance: a combination of productivity and supply effects, which warrants explicit attention. The effect manifests itself in the form of the student's starting point at the beginning of the year following contact with the previous teacher. A student whose teacher in period $t - 1$ did a good job will start period t at a higher level than would otherwise be the case. Of course, a teacher doing a "bad" job can have the opposite effect. This effect on subsequent starting points is a potentially important means by which teachers exercise intertemporal influences on their students.

Set of Previous Teachers. The mechanisms described above, through which the immediate past teacher has impact on the subsequent performance of students, also pertain to teachers from the student's more distant past. It is not obvious a priori, however, whether the effects of the broader set will be larger or smaller than the effects of the immediate past teacher. One reason for expecting the effect to be smaller is that time has not had a chance to erode the magnitude of the immediate past teacher's influence. A second reason is that previous teachers' lagged influences may tend to offset one another. In other words, the set may contain one teacher who had a powerful positive influence over time as well as one teacher who had a powerful negative influence over time. Under these circumstances, the collective effect of the two teachers will be smaller than the effect of either teacher looked at individually.

In contrast, the fact that teachers are likely to vary in the magnitude of their influence over time, coupled with the realization that the most influential teacher need not be the most recently experienced teacher, makes it less obvious that the effects of the set will be smaller than the effects of the most recent teacher.

The effects of the set of previous teachers may be large because they will encompass whatever tendency there is for lagged influences to accumulate and become magnified over time. The potential for a good performance on the part of a teacher or a sequence of teachers to accumulate and lead to magnified positive effects for students must be balanced against the potential for bad performances to have similarly magnified negative effects.

Moreover, attributes of the set can capture new information about a student's past experiences with teachers, and this added information could provide useful insights into what makes important differences for students. For example, using the set, we can distinguish between students on the basis of how many different teachers they experienced over a period of time. We can also use the set to characterize the variability and sequencing of past teachers.

School-Level Set of Teachers. School-level teaching resources can be thought of as a resource stock that is available to both teachers and students within each school. We can discern productivity, as well as supply, effects that are relevant to both teachers and students, but, as we indicate below, it is not likely that either of these effects will be large in magnitude.

Productivity Effects. It is possible for an individual teacher to improve his or her effectiveness by drawing on the experience of and advice available from colleagues. Being surrounded by more capable teachers who are willing to help an individual teacher could facilitate significant improvement in that teacher's performance. These improvements, to the degree that they arise, constitute productivity effects for that particular teacher that stem from school-level teaching resources.

Of course, realization of these effects presupposes both a willingness to receive and a willingness (and ability) to provide the requisite assistance. The day-to-day press of activities in schools can seriously interfere with this kind of exchange taking place, and it will likely limit the magnitude of the school-level effects that can be observed.[5] Rather than attempt to analyze the dynamics of the actual assistance that is forthcoming, we think of the school-level teaching resource as a stock and characterize it in terms of its mean and internal variability. We are interested in seeing if this resource stock has an effect on the productivity of proximate teaching resources.

Supply effects. Students can also draw on these school-level resources by seeking help from a teacher other than the proximate teacher. Alternatively, a school may make efforts to supply these resources by institutionalizing tutoring or other kinds of study assistance programs. The defining characteristic is that a teacher other than the student's own (i.e., proximate) supplies an instructional resource.

Just as is the case for teachers, students will vary in their willingness and ability to draw on and make productive use of these resources.

Moreover, teachers will certainly vary in their willingness to provide assistance to other than their assigned students. It would be a significant undertaking to analyze the underlying decision-making processes involved here, and it is not obvious that the effort is warranted given the modest degree to which this kind of teaching assistance can be observed in schools. For now, we are content to characterize the school-level stock in terms of selected mean and variability statistics. We are interested in seeing if differences in the character of the available stock makes a difference in pupil performance.

NARROWING THE TEACHER RESOURCE CONCEPTUALIZATION

For the purpose of our empirical analyses, we focus our attention on the subject-matter preparation of secondary teachers in the areas of mathematics and science. Our choice is dictated partly by promising earlier studies of the determinants of teacher effectiveness and partly by the availability of data.

There is a growing body of research suggesting that measures of what teachers know and can do have important implications for the performance gains of students. The Equality of Educational Opportunity (EEO) survey (Coleman et al. 1966) was one of the earliest studies to find positive relationships between measures of teachers' verbal abilities and pupil performance, although, strictly speaking, this study did not examine learning gains of pupils.[6] More recently, analysts have considered other dimensions of the capabilities teachers bring to classrooms. For example, Ferguson (1991) included measures of teacher literacy in his assessment of educational quality in a study of Texas school district productivity and concluded that differences in the quality of schooling account for between one-quarter and one-third of the district variation in student test scores.

Hanushek, Gomes-Neto, and Harbison (1992) had access to measures of teacher subject-matter knowledge in their Brazilian data and found evidence of positive relationships between how much a teacher knew about what was being taught and their students' subject-specific learning gains. In contrast to the EEO and the Ferguson studies, Hanushek and his colleagues focused their attention more on how much a teacher knew about what was being taught than on the teacher's ability to learn or process information.[7]

In our earlier analyses (Monk 1994), we took advantage of a data set that provides detailed information about the subject-matter preparation of a nationally representative sample of secondary science and mathematics teachers in U.S. high schools. We found evidence of positive relationships between the number of subject-related courses in a teacher's background and subsequent performance gains of these teachers' students within the indicated subject area. While we lacked direct measures of how much the teachers in our sample actually understood about the subject being taught, our findings are consistent with the general proposition that what teachers know and can do has implications for how much learning takes place within classrooms.

While our focus is on subject-matter preparation, many of the arguments we make for considering the collective effects of faculties are quite general and would apply to more direct measures of what teachers actually know and can accomplish, as well as to other, broader measures of teacher attributes. The level of teacher experience within a school counts as one of these alternative teacher attributes, and we have included it in our attempt to identify the direct, as well as the lagged, effects of both the proximate and the immediate past teacher.

We focus on mathematics and science subject-matter preparation partly because of the high interest policymakers are showing in these areas of the curriculum and partly because these subjects are the focus of our data. The secondary school choice is similarly dictated partly by policymaking implications and partly by the nature of the available data.

Data and Methods

The Longitudinal Study of American Youth (LSAY) is a panel survey of American middle and high school science and mathematics education. The collection began in the fall of 1987, and the results reported here are based on the original collection plus the first, second, and third follow-up surveys as well as information collected in the spring of 1991. All of the data come from the April 1992 public use release.

The base-year sample consists of 2,831 students who were enrolled in the tenth grade in the fall of 1987. These students were drawn from fifty-one randomly selected localities from around the nation. The sample consists entirely of public schools that were selected randomly with probabilities proportional to the enrollment size within twelve sampling strata. The strata were defined in terms of geographic region (four categories) and community type (urban, suburban, rural). Sixty tenth-grade students were randomly selected from within each school in the study.

Survey instruments were completed by the sampled students, their teachers, their principals, and their parents. In addition, achievement tests that focused on mathematics and science knowledge were administered in the falls of 1987, 1988, and 1989.

MEASURES OF STUDENT ACHIEVEMENT

The achievement tests utilize items developed by the National Assessment of Educational Progress (NAEP). The NAEP items permit an assessment of students' capabilities along several dimensions of cognitive achievement, including several higher-order skills.

The focus in this study is on the composite measures of student performance in mathematics and science. Both composite scores were estimated using item response methods, which recognize that some items on a testing instrument are more difficult than others. Students' response patterns were adjusted in light of these variable difficulty levels. The 1992 release contains a series of scores that includes imputed values for students who missed a portion of the testing sequence. We experimented with using the imputed values versus other reported scores and found few substantive differences. The results reported here are based on the imputed values. The reliability coefficient for the mathematics composite score in 1987 was .92; in the 1988 administration it was .95. The corresponding coefficients for science were .85 and .91.

TEACHER SURVEY

All science and mathematics teachers in the sampled schools were asked to complete a general survey asking for background information. The resulting teacher file provides information about the number of undergraduate and graduate courses taken within various areas of the curriculum. Within mathematics, no subject-specific breakdown was requested. Within science, teachers reported courses taken in specific subjects (e.g., chemistry, biology). We organized these specific subjects into two broad types of science: life science and physical science. In addition, teachers were asked to distinguish between undergraduate and graduate courses in both mathematics and science. We collapsed these into single counts of courses in the respective subject areas: mathematics, life science, and physical science.

Teachers were asked to report the number of both semester and quarter courses in their preparation. This feature of the data created a number of difficulties. First, some of the teachers reported credit hours rather than course counts. This was a particularly serious problem in the earlier release of the data. In our previous work (Monk 1994), we developed a method for combining quarter and semester courses to yield a total course count. The results reported here rely on the progress the LSAY staff has made toward refining these data and clarifying instances where suspect cases arose. The 1992 release included LSAY-supplied counts of teacher courses, and we relied on these exclusively.

Methods had to be developed for handling missing information about teacher course-taking behavior. It was common for teachers to fill in only those sections of the questionnaire where they had courses to report. Thus, treating blanks as missing data would seriously distort the information being received since, in these cases, the blank is equivalent to a zero response. Our method for handling this difficulty involved distinguishing teachers who reported no course-taking information from the remainder of the sample. Teachers who reported no information were considered missing. Blanks within a record of a teacher who reported some course-taking information were recoded as zeros.

We linked student information with the relevant teacher information by using course-specific teacher identification codes. The school-level aggregates we used reflect the characteristics of the subject-specific faculties. Thus, when we speak of the school mean level of course preparation in mathematics, we are referring to the average for those who considered themselves to be mathematics teachers.

MULTIPLE LEVELS

We distinguished explicitly among the proximate teacher, the immediate past teacher, the set of previous teachers, and the set of all subject-matter specialists in the school. The proximate teacher is the teacher teaching the student at the beginning of the indicated school year (sophomore or junior). The immediate past teacher is the teacher who taught the student at the beginning of the previous school year. Thus, for the junior year, the immediate past teacher is the teacher the student experienced at the beginning of the sophomore year.

The set of previous teachers consists of all teachers assigned to the student in the indicated subject area during the sophomore and junior years, including the proximate teacher. The proximate teacher is included in this set partly because of data availability problems (excluding the proximate teacher would have reduced our set to a single teacher in some cases)[8] and partly because there is a real sense in which a proximate teacher is a previous teacher. Recall that we defined the proximate teacher to be an individual teacher who has primary responsibility for a given student's instruction at an instant in time. If that point is defined as the end of the junior year, the same teacher could count as both the immediate past teacher (during the earlier portion of the junior year) and the proximate teacher.

The set of all subject-matter specialists in the school also includes the proximate teacher.

ESTIMATION ISSUES

We rely on ordinary least squares (OLS) estimating techniques throughout these analyses. We considered the use of random effect statistical models such as the increasingly popular hierarchical linear model (HLM) (Bryk and Raudenbush 1992), but encountered several interrelated problems. First, our conceptualization of different levels creates an interpretation problem for an HLM analysis because the conventional HLM places emphasis on the nested nature of levels. However, in our case, two students from different schools could be assigned to the same second-level group if their previous teachers were sufficiently similar. Second, if we imposed a further restriction that included the identity of the school, we would have faced unacceptably small numbers of observations within each grouping. Finally, we discovered early in our data analyses that the overwhelming amount of variation in pupil performance existed within, and not across, schools.[9] This empirical result, in part, prompted our interest in differentiating among levels within schools.

We do not claim that the OLS results we report here necessarily overcome or solve these difficulties, but we see problems with the application of the HLM and believe it is more prudent to rely on simpler methods at this early stage of the inquiry.

The oversampling of students in small schools makes it necessary to employ weights in the student-level analyses. We scaled the weights so that they do not artificially inflate the degrees of freedom in the analyses.

Means and standard deviations for our key variables appear in the appendix to this chapter.

FINDINGS

All of the production function models we estimate have a value-added form and include a pretest score among the predictors of a gain score.[10] We are less interested in estimating the complete education production function than we are in gaining insight into the multilevel effects of selected teacher attributes. We have separated our findings according to the time period: sophomore-year gain, junior-year gain, and total gain over the sophomore and junior years. We have also dealt separately with the mathematics and science subject areas. And we have looked separately at production functions for high- and low-performing students.

There are a number of different ways to estimate the multilevel teacher resource effects that we have identified. We begin by examining the effects of both the proximate and the immediate past teacher, and then broaden the focus to include the effects of all the previous teachers we could observe as well as the collective effects of each school's faculty as a whole.

PROXIMATE AND IMMEDIATE PAST TEACHER EFFECTS

The results of regressing various gain scores in mathematics on alternative combinations of student and teacher attributes are reported in Table 2.1. The results pertain to those students enrolled in both a sophomore- and a junior-year mathematics course. For these students, the pretest score has a negative effect on the gain score. This is consistent with other applications of this kind of model[11] and suggests that ceiling effects are present. Students starting at higher performance levels tend to experience less growth than do their otherwise comparable classmates beginning the year at relatively low performance levels. These effects occur for all three time periods under study. It is interesting to note that they occur during the junior year and over the two-year period even when the sample is restricted to the high-performing students.

The dummy variables representing the type of course being studied have significant effects on pupils' gain scores.[12] Being enrolled in an advanced sophomore mathematics course has a positive effect, while being enrolled in a remedial sophomore course has the opposite effect. These effects are present when controls are in place for both the students' pretest scores and socioeconomic status (SES), so it seems that we are picking up more than simple selection effects. It appears that two students with the same pretest scores and SES would realize different gains depending on the type of course in which they are placed. It may be that teachers cover more curriculum in advanced courses and less in remedial courses. Or it may be that the quality of teaching varies in the indicated direction.

In this light, it is worth noting that in the whole-sample models, the positive coefficients for placement in an advanced course tend to be smaller in absolute value than the negative coefficients for placement in

Table 2.1. Effects of Proximate and Immediate Past Teacher Preparation Levels on Student Performance Gains in Mathematics (OLS Regression Coefficients)

	Sophomore Gain			Junior Gain					Total Gain				
	Whole Sample	High[a] Pretest	Low[b] Pretest	Whole Sample	Whole Sample	Whole Sample	High Pretest	Low Pretest	Whole Sample	Whole Sample	Whole Sample	High Pretest	Low Pretest
Intercept	12.17*** (.85)	3.28* (1.85)	12.02*** (1.56)	9.96*** (1.11)	8.38*** (1.14)	9.46*** (1.29)	16.37*** (2.00)	11.92*** (2.24)	15.56*** (1.24)	14.34*** (1.30)	15.31*** (1.45)	10.08*** (2.72)	18.16*** (2.99)
Soph. pretest	-.15*** (.01)	-.03 (.03)	-.14*** (.03)						-.18*** (.02)	-.16*** (.02)	-.17*** (.02)	-.10*** (.04)	-.23*** (.05)
Junior pretest				-.14*** (.02)	-.11*** (.02)	-.12*** (.02)	-.21*** (.03)	-.19*** (.04)					
Soph. remedial course	-2.00*** (.35)	-2.13*** (.81)	-2.24*** (.43)	-.70*** (.49)	-1.44*** (.51)	-2.06*** (.56)	-1.37 (1.70)	-1.17* (.69)	-2.52*** (.56)	-2.51*** (.59)	-2.93*** (.65)	-1.43 (1.92)	-3.00*** (.84)
Soph. advanced course	1.47*** (.48)	.83* (.45)	4.80*** (1.55)	.82 (.54)	.79 (.60)	.46 (.63)	.46 (.59)	-.33 (2.81)	1.10* (.62)	1.04 (.70)	.72 (.73)	.50 (.67)	3.25 (3.45)
SES	.24 (.18)	.12 (.22)	.23 (.28)	.63*** (.21)	.60*** (.21)	.55*** (.23)	.24 (.28)	.91** (.39)	.44* (.24)	.49* (.25)	.49* (.27)	.20 (.32)	.96** (.48)
Soph. proximate teacher's prep.	.04* (.02)	.06** (.02)	.02 (.03)	-.00 (.02)		.02 (.03)	-.01 (.03)	.08 (.05)	.01 (.03)		.06* (.03)	.03 (.04)	.10* (.06)
Soph. proximate teacher's experience	-.01 (.01)	-.01 (.02)	-.01 (.02)	.02 (.02)		-.02 (.02)	.03 (.02)	-.02 (.04)	.00 (.02)		-.01 (.02)	.02 (.03)	-.05 (.05)
Junior proximate teacher's prep.					.00 (.02)	-.00 (.03)	-.03 (.04)	.02 (.05)		.00 (.03)	-.01 (.03)	-.04 (.04)	.01 (.06)
Junior proximate teacher's experience					-.01 (.02)	-.03 (.03)	-.02 (.03)	-.02 (.04)		-.01 (.02)	-.01 (.03)	.01 (.03)	-.02 (.05)
N	1,955	1,028	927	1,254	1,175	977	597	380	1,253	1,175	977	597	380
R²(a)	.07	.01	.05	.05	.03	.04	.08	.07	.06	.05	.06	.00	.07

Note: Figures in parentheses represent standard errors.
[a] ≥ median, 61.41
[b] < median, 61.41
*p < .10   **p < .05   ***p < .01

a remedial course. Indeed, in several junior- and total-gain specifications, the coefficient for the advanced course dummy falls short of statistical significance. In contrast, the remedial coefficients are consistently negative and statistically significant across all of the whole-sample specifications. This kind of inequality in absolute value suggests that it costs students more to be placed in a remedial setting than it benefits students to be placed in an advanced setting.

Notice, also, the relatively large positive coefficient for placement in an advanced sophomore class for low-pretest students. This finding suggests that the pretest score may have less to do with the potential for performance gains than is widely supposed. No comparable effect can be discerned for the junior year, but the sophomore-year effect is large enough to generate a positive result in the two-year-gain model.

SES has a statistically significant positive effect only for the junior year. The absence of an SES effect during the sophomore year is surprising, but the junior year effect is sufficiently strong to register a positive effect for growth over the two years. It is interesting to notice that the SES effect is stronger for the low-pretest subsample of students. The relative strength of this SES effect for low-pretest students can also be seen in the sophomore year results, although here the effect for the low-pretest students falls short of statistical significance.

Turning now to the teachers' attributes, we find a small positive direct effect of the proximate teacher's subject-matter preparation during the sophomore year for the high-pretest students. This positive effect can also be found for the whole sample where the gain in performance is measured over two years. What is interesting here is that the sophomore teacher effect can be discerned only when the attributes for the junior-year teacher are entered simultaneously. Moreover, when we looked explicitly at the lagged effect of the sophomore teacher on pupil gains during the junior year, we found nothing. The effect of the proximate teacher's subject-matter preparation during the junior year had a similarly negligible effect.

There is also an interesting change between the sophomore-year and the two-year model in the type of student showing the effect of the subject-matter preparation of the sophomore teacher. During the sophomore year, the proximate teacher's preparation has a positive effect for the high-pretest students. For the two-year-gain models, the positive effect is limited to the low-pretest students. The appearance of an effect within the two-year model for the low-pretest students may be related to the extra time these students may require before they are able to realize the benefits of teacher subject-matter preparation. In highly sequential courses like mathematics, this kind of delayed effect may be particularly important for those low-pretest students who continue to study the subject. It is less clear why the effect for the high-pretest students disappears in the two-year-gain model.

Teacher experience, the second teacher attribute we examined, had little impact on pupils' gain scores in mathematics regardless of the year or type of student.

In Table 2.2, our focus shifts to students' performance gains in science. These analyses closely parallel what we reported for mathematics except for the distinction between types of subject-matter preparation. Our earlier findings demonstrated the importance of the difference between life and physical science preparation levels for secondary science teachers (Monk 1994), and we maintain this distinction here.

The pretest coefficients are negative and are of roughly the same magnitude as those we found for mathematics, thus they can be interpreted in the same way. The dummy variables for type of course have effects that are similar to what we saw for mathematics except that here the absolute values for the advanced courses tend to be comparable to or larger than those for the remedial courses.[13] This is the reverse of the result for mathematics.

In contrast to the mathematics results where there was no evidence of an SES effect during the sophomore year, Table 2.2 reveals a positive SES effect for sophomores with high pretest scores. These positive effects carry over into the junior year but are largely lost in the two-year-gain models. We note with interest the evidence suggesting that in science, it is the high-pretest students for whom SES makes a difference. Recall that, in mathematics, the SES effect—where it could be observed—was more connected to low-pretest students.

The effects of teacher subject-matter preparation in science are interesting and contrast with what we found for mathematics. In general, our measures of teacher preparation in the life sciences have no significant effects on pupil performance. This holds for both the proximate and the immediate past teacher and pertains to both the sophomore and the junior year. The result also holds for the two-year-gain model.

In contrast, we find evidence of a positive effect of physical science preparation on the part of the sophomore-year teacher for the high-pretest students. Moreover, in addition to the proximate effect for the high-pretest sophomores, there is evidence of a positive lagged effect during the subsequent junior year for the whole sample. However, the lagged effect is modest in size and is lost once the attributes of the junior-

Table 2.2. Effects of Proximate and Immediate Past Teacher Preparation Levels on Student Performance Gains in Science (OLS Regression Coefficients)

	Sophomore Gain			Junior Gain					Total Gain				
	Whole Sample[a]	High Pretest	Low Pretest[b]	Whole Sample	Whole Sample	Whole Sample	High Pretest	Low Pretest	Whole Sample	Whole Sample	Whole Sample	High Pretest	Low Pretest
Intercept	13.87** (.92)	18.59*** (1.94)	3.69* (2.04)	10.43*** (1.33)	11.47*** (1.31)	12.15*** (1.56)	15.20*** (2.55)	18.65*** (2.58)	18.51*** (1.37)	18.82*** (1.38)	20.56*** (1.63)	19.26*** (2.96)	16.63*** (4.02)
Soph. pretest	-.16*** (.01)	-.24*** (.03)	.04 (.04)						-.20*** (.02)	-.21*** (.02)	-.23*** (.02)	-.22*** (.04)	-.13* (.08)
Junior pretest				-.15*** (.02)	-.15*** (.02)	-.16*** (.02)	-.20*** (.03)	-.28*** (.04)					
Soph. remedial course	-.98** (.39)	.99* (.59)	-2.00*** (.53)	.08 (.57)	-.16 (.56)	-.25 (.63)	-.26 (.90)	.07 (.92)	-1.48** (.63)	-.90 (.63)	-1.06 (.70)	.94 (1.00)	-2.74** (1.08)
Soph. advanced course	1.22** (.48)	1.85*** (.49)	1.71 (1.14)	.82 (.56)	1.08** (.50)	1.07* (.59)	1.01 (.63)	-1.67 (1.62)	1.13* (.62)	1.13** (.56)	1.42** (.66)	1.85*** (.69)	.00 (1.92)
SES	.27 (.19)	.57** (.24)	-.03 (.30)	.12 (.25)	.62** (.26)	.49* (.28)	.13 (.35)	.51 (.45)	.13 (.28)	.51* (.29)	.44 (.32)	.54 (.39)	.23 (.54)
Soph. proximate teacher's life science prep.	-.00 (.02)	.02 (.02)	-.04 (.03)	-.00 (.02)	-.01 (.02)	-.01 (.02)	-.01 (.03)	.00 (.04)	-.01 (.03)	-.01 (.03)	-.01 (.03)	.00 (.03)	-.02 (.05)

Table (rotated 90°). Regression coefficients with standard errors in parentheses.

	1	2	3	4	5	6	7	8	9	10	11	12	13
Soph. proximate teacher's physical science prep.	.02 (.02)	.04* (.02)	.01 (.04)	.05* (.03)			.05 (.03)				.03 (.03)	.03 (.04)	.06 (.06)
Soph. proximate teacher's experience	−.00 (.02)	−.06*** (.02)	.06** (.02)	−.01 (.02)		−.04 (.03)	−.04* (.02)	−.00 (.05)			−.05** (.03)	−.07** (.03)	−.04 (.04)
Junior proximate teacher's life science prep.					−.04 (.03)	−.05 (.03)		−.07 (.05)	−.03 (.03)		−.05 (.03)	−.03 (.04)	−.07 (.06)
Junior proximate teacher's physical science prep.					−.04 (.03)	−.06** (.03)		−.08 (.05)	−.01 (.03)		−.02 (.03)	−.00 (.04)	−.07 (.06)
Junior proximate teacher's experience					.02 (.02)	.02 (.02)		.04 (.04)	.02 (.02)		.02 (.02)	.03 (.03)	.02 (.04)
N	1,936	1,044	892	1,066	1,045	912	1,066	316	1,045	1,066	912	596	316
R²(a)	.06	.07	.02	.05	.06	.06	.07	.15	.08	.08	.08	.04	.01

Note: Figures in parentheses represent standard errors.

[a] ≥ median, 56.84
[b] < median, 56.84

* $p < .10$ ** $p < .05$ *** $p < .01$

year teacher are introduced. A lagged positive effect of the sophomore teacher is also not detectable in the two-year-gain model.

It is puzzling to note that subject-matter preparation in the physical sciences on the part of the junior-year teacher has a negative effect on pupil gains during the junior year. This sign reversal between the junior and sophomore years for the proximate science teacher's preparation in the physical sciences is consistent with our earlier analyses where we looked in more detail at proximate teacher effects (Monk 1994).

The experience level of the proximate teacher has negative effects for high-pretest students and positive effects for low-pretest students during the sophomore year. This is the reverse of the interaction found years ago by Summers and Wolfe (1977) in their study of urban elementary pupils. The effect is sufficiently strong to manifest itself in the two-year-gain model but does not appear to have any lagged effect during the junior year. Moreover, the experience level of the junior-year proximate teacher makes no difference in terms of pupil performance.

The results we report in Tables 2.1 and 2.2 contain only the slightest hint of lagged teacher subject-matter preparation effects. The lagged effect we found was limited to science, was small in magnitude, and was quite unstable. However, there are other ways in which the subject-matter preparation of a teacher in one period can affect pupil progress during later periods. Recall our interest in what we called the combination effect where students were able to start a subsequent period at a higher level of performance than would otherwise have been possible because of the work of their previous teacher. Also recall the potential for the previous teacher to affect the productivity of subsequently supplied resources. We can gain insight into these effects by dividing the students taking junior-year courses on the basis of their immediate past teacher's subject-matter preparation level. If these effects are real, they can manifest themselves in the form of different intercepts and slope coefficients for the junior-year teaching resource. Tables 2.3 and 2.4 report the results of these comparisons for mathematics and science, respectively.

Table 2.3 reveals a positive difference between the intercepts estimated for the junior-year students in mathematics. The intercept coefficient for those students whose sophomore-year teacher possessed relatively high levels of subject-matter preparation in mathematics (≥ 9 mathematics courses) was 10.61. The corresponding figure for juniors whose sophomore-year teacher possessed relatively low levels of subject-matter preparation was 6.82. The differences between these two regression models are statistically significant at better than the .01 level.

Table 2.3 also reveals separate estimates of the marginal productivities

Table 2.3. *Junior-Year Performance Gains in Mathematics by Subject-Matter Preparation Levels of the Immediate Past Teacher (OLS Regression Coefficients)*

	All	High-Prep. Soph. Proximate Teacher[a]	Low-Prep. Soph. Proximate Teacher[b]
Intercept	8.96***	10.61***	6.82***
	(1.13)	(1.42)	(1.96)
Junior pretest	−.12***	−.13***	−.10***
	(.02)	(.02)	(.03)
Junior remedial course	−1.39***	−2.65***	.08
	(.47)	(.62)	(.73)
Junior advanced course	1.73***	1.57***	2.19**
	(.50)	(.58)	(.94)
SES	.54**	.38	.83**
	(.21)	(.26)	(.37)
Junior proximate teacher's preparation	−.01	−.05	.04
	(.02)	(.03)	(.04)
Junior proximate teacher's experience	−.01	−.01	.01
	(.02)	(.02)	(.03)
N	1,175	742	433
R^2	.04	.06	.03

Note: Figures in parentheses represent standard errors.
[a] ≥ median, 9
[b] < median, 9
*p < .10   **p < .05   ***p < .01

of subject-matter preparation and experience for the proximate (junior-year) teacher for students with low- and high-preparation sophomore-year teachers. The previous year's teacher's preparation level has no apparent effect on the effectiveness of these two attributes of the junior-year teacher.

Table 2.4 reports a parallel analysis for science. Unlike the results for mathematics, there were no discernible differences in the effects of the sophomore-year science teacher's subject-matter preparation on the estimated intercepts for these models. However, there is some evidence of a difference on the effect of the proximate teacher's life science preparation. The negative effect of teacher life science preparation on pupil performance gains during the junior year is mitigated to some degree by the level of science preparation resident within the previous year's teacher. However, the differences between the models are slight and fall short of statistical significance at the .01 level.

Table 2.4. Junior-Year Performance Gains in Science by Subject-Matter
Preparation Levels of the Immediate Past Teacher (OLS Regression Coefficients)

	All	High-Prep. Soph. Proximate Teacher[a]	Low-Prep. Soph. Proximate Teacher[b]
Intercept	10.78***	10.58***	10.78***
	(1.31)	(1.71)	(2.12)
Junior pretest	−.15***	−.15***	−.14***
	(.02)	(.03)	(.03)
Junior remedial course	.43	.59	.45
	(.48)	(.62)	(.83)
Junior advanced course	.89*	1.55***	.06
	(.47)	(.58)	(.85)
SES	.64**	.50	.81**
	(.26)	(.34)	(.41)
Junior proximate teacher's life science prep.	−.04	−.03	−.09*
	(.03)	(.03)	(.05)
Junior proximate teacher's physical science prep.	−.03	−.04	.02
	(.03)	(.03)	(.05)
Junior proximate teacher's experience	.02	.03	.01
	(.02)	(.02)	(.03)
N	1,045	677	368
R^2	.06	.05	.06

Note: Figures in parentheses represent errors.
[a] ≥ median, 15
[b] < median, 15
*$p < .10$ **$p < .05$ ***$p < .01$

SETS OF PREVIOUS TEACHERS AND SCHOOL-LEVEL SUBJECT-MATTER SPECIALISTS

The final step in our analysis shifts away from the individual proximate and immediate past teachers to the two collective types of nonproximate teachers we have identified: the set of a student's previous teachers and the set of all subject-matter specialists within a given school. We conducted two types of analysis. First, in order to determine whether the school-level set of subject-matter specialists had any effect on the productivities of proximate teachers, we carried out the kind of analysis we reported in Tables 2.3 and 2.4. This involved dividing the sample on the basis of the mean school-level subject preparation levels and checking to see if there was any evidence suggesting that teachers were more productive in school settings where their colleagues were better trained. The fact that we found no such evidence is not surprising given the difficulties associated with fostering and maintaining meaningful levels of collegial support among teachers (Johnson 1990).

Second, we estimated production functions at the individual student level and included variables measuring selected properties of these two sets. Because of the focus here on "school"-level variables, we excluded those students enrolled in noncomparable school settings. Specifically, we excluded students whose secondary school encompassed more than grades nine through twelve.[14] Because the analyses encompass all of the remaining students in the sample, including those who did not enroll in a junior-year course, we added a control variable for the number of semesters of courses taken. Tables 2.5 and 2.6 report our findings for the mathematics and science subject areas, respectively. Both tables deal exclusively with the two-year period that covers the sophomore and junior years.

In Table 2.5, we find that student attributes such as the type of course taken during the sophomore year and the number of semesters of courses taken have the expected effects on pupil gains. We observed similar results in Table 2.1 where placement in an advanced (remedial) course had a positive (negative) impact on performance gains. We also see again the tendency for the magnitude of the remedial course coefficient to be larger in absolute value than that of the advanced course coefficient. But notice again the interesting exception to this pattern when we look only at the low-pretest students.

The number of semesters of courses is a crude measure of exposure to mathematics instruction and has consistently positive and statistically significant effects on pupils' gain scores, although the magnitude of the effect appears to be modest. Using the mean senior score as the basis for calculating a percentage effect, having one more semester of a mathematics course translates into a 1.5 percent improvement in performance, according to the whole-sample model showing the largest impact. We also found that the strength of this relationship is not restricted to either the high- or low-pretest students. Both types of students appear to benefit from increased amounts of mathematics instruction.

These findings are consistent with the results of other production function studies where it has been demonstrated that the increases in the amount of time students devote to their study of a subject pay dividends in terms of performance gains (e.g., Brown and Saks 1987).

Table 2.5 also reports the results of regressing summary measures of the preparation characteristics of each student's set of previous mathematics teachers over the two years. There is an overall positive effect of the student-specific set mean on performance gains. However, the effect is confined to the low-pretest portion of the sample.

The effects of variation among each student's previous teachers also

Table 2.5. Effects of Student Specific and School-Level Sets of Teacher Preparation on Student Performance Gains in Mathematics over Two Years
(OLS Regression Coefficients)

	Whole Sample			High Pretest[a]			Low Pretest[b]		
Intercept	12.52***	12.01***	12.56***	7.98***	9.50***	8.37***	15.76***	13.61***	15.34***
	(1.19)	(1.27)	(1.39)	(2.67)	(2.60)	(2.80)	(1.99)	(2.17)	(2.34)
Soph. pretest	-.19***	-.17***	-.19***	-.13***	-.12***	-.12***	-.26***	-.21***	-.25***
	(.02)	(.02)	(.02)	(.04)	(.03)	(.04)	(.03)	(.03)	(.03)
Soph. remedial course	-2.16***	-2.28***	-2.07***	-2.22**	-2.41**	-2.25*	-2.08***	-2.21***	-1.93***
	(.46)	(.43)	(.46)	(1.18)	(1.13)	(1.19)	(.54)	(.50)	(.55)
Soph. advanced course	1.76***	1.55**	1.52**	1.13*	1.10*	.99	4.52**	4.25**	4.14**
	(.61)	(.62)	(.63)	(.62)	(.62)	(.64)	(1.86)	(1.89)	(1.87)
SES	.45**	.38*	.46**	.08	.21	.11	.77**	.50	.78**
	(.23)	(.22)	(.24)	(.30)	(.29)	(.31)	(.35)	(.33)	(.35)
No. of semesters of math taken	.94***	.73***	.87***	.92***	.69***	.88***	.91***	.77***	.82**
	(.22)	(.15)	(.22)	(.30)	(.20)	(.30)	(.33)	(.22)	(.33)

Student-specific set									
Mean prep.	.07**		.11***	.02		.05	.13***		.17***
	(.03)		(.04)	(.04)		(.05)	(.05)		(.05)
Std. dev. of prep.	−.04		−.05	−.17*		−.18**	.06		.04
	(.07)		(.07)	(.09)		(.09)	(.10)		(.10)
No. of teachers	−.26		−.25	.37		.39	−.69		−.70
	(.34)		(.35)	(.49)		(.50)	(.49)		(.49)
School-level set									
Mean prep.		−.02	−.11		−.00	−.04		−.03	−.14
		(.06)	(.07)		(.08)	(.09)		(.10)	(.11)
Std. dev. of prep.		−.03	−.04		−.02	−.06		−.05	−.01
		(.10)	(.10)		(.13)	(.13)		(.15)	(.17)
No. of teachers		.04	.07*		−.00	.02		.08	.12**
		(.04)	(.04)		(.05)	(.05)		(.06)	(.06)
N	1,717	1,907	1,717	896	967	896	821	940	821
R^2	.07	.06	.08	.03	.02	.03	.09	.07	.10

Note: Figures in parentheses represent standard errors.

[a] ≥ median, 61.41

[b] < median, 61.41

*p < .10   **p < .05   ***p < .01

depend on whether the student is high or low scoring on the pretest. For high-scoring students, there is a negative effect; for low-scoring students, there is no effect. This dependence on the student's pretest may be related to the underlying distribution of teachers across teaching assignments. In a series of ongoing analyses, we are finding that high-pretest students tend to be assigned teachers with higher levels of subject-matter preparation. For these students, higher levels of variation within their set may be picking up the effects of the presence of unusually poorly prepared teachers. The effect is nevertheless puzzling since one might suppose that high-pretest students, other things being equal, would be more resilient to the negative effects of a poorly prepared teacher.

Our counts of the number of different teachers within each student's previous set stemmed from an interest in seeing if aspects of disruption in an instructional program have negative effects on pupil performance. The number of different teachers has no independent effect on performance when a control is present for the number of different semesters of mathematics taken by the student. We also experimented with variables measuring aspects of the sequencing of teachers. For example, we looked to see if having a series of teachers where subject-matter preparation increases over time has an independent effect. We found no evidence of this sort of sequencing effect, although the short period of time we are working with needs to be kept in mind.

The final block of variables in Table 2.5 captures aspects of the subject-specific faculty within each student's school. These variables measure the school-level set of teacher resources, and the only effect we were able to discern from this source was the count of faculty comprising the set. For low-pretest students, having a larger faculty has a positive effect on performance gains. The effect appears only in the models containing all of the different attributes we have been considering. Perhaps the most plausible interpretation is related to the presumed greater availability of more specialized courses from larger, compared to smaller, mathematics faculties. Monk and Haller (1993) found that the incidence of both remedial and advanced specialized courses in mathematics increases with secondary school size. The fact that the effect is confined to the low-pretest students is less easy to explain. It may be that these students are more dependent on teacher-provided resources, but this contradicts the argument we advanced above regarding the greater sensitivity of high-pretest students to variability in the preparation levels of their teachers.

Finally, in Table 2.6 we report a parallel analysis for science performance gains. The results for the pretest, course placement, and quantity of instruction variables are similar to what we have seen in previous tables.

In contrast to what we found for mathematics, there is little evidence of cumulative effects of the mean preparation level of each student's set of previous science teachers. Neither the mean life science course count nor the mean physical science course count makes any difference in terms of pupil performance gains. The only effect of the student-specific set that we found involves the degree of variation in the level of life science preparation. It has a small positive effect that manifests for only the high-pretest students.

Table 2.6 also reports the effects of the school-level set on pupil performance gains in science. It is interesting to notice that more school-level effects can be found in science than in mathematics. In particular, the table reveals a positive relationship between the mean level of physical science preparation that is embodied in the school's faculty and the performance gains realized by low-pretest students. There is no comparable effect for the high-pretest subsample, but the effect for the low-pretest students is sufficiently strong to manifest itself in the result for the whole sample. We can also observe some evidence of a negative effect associated with the mean level of life science preparation on the part of the school's faculty. However, this effect is lost when controls are in place for the students' previous teachers, and it cannot be observed for the whole-sample version of the model.

The table suggests that the level of variability within a school's faculty can also makè a difference. High variability in the level of life science preparation has a positive impact on high-pretest students, while high variability in the level of physical science preparation has a negative impact on low-pretest students. We suspect the explanation for these reversals lies in the underlying allocation of teachers across teaching assignments. It may also be related to the differential ability of high- and low-pretest students to benefit from teachers with life, compared with physical, science backgrounds.

DISCUSSION

We have sought to identify a series of teacher resource levels that exist within, as well as across, schooling units. Our goal has been to establish conceptually the reasons for expecting effects at each of these levels and to provide greater clarity about how the levels interact. These are important considerations given the increasing emphasis on the school as the focal point of efforts to address concerns over both efficiency and equity. We need to move beyond simple distinctions between school and

Table 2.6. *Effects of Student-Specific and School-Level Sets of Teacher Preparation on Student Performance Gains in Science over Two Years (OLS Regression Coefficients)*

	Whole Sample			High Pretest[a]			Low Pretest[b]		
Intercept	14.63***	13.65***	13.60***	13.44***	12.18***	11.25***	11.56***	12.26***	12.08***
	(1.22)	(1.22)	(1.49)	(2.38)	(2.29)	(2.65)	(2.68)	(2.50)	(3.00)
Soph. pretest	−.19***	−.18***	−.19***	−.19***	−.17***	−.18***	−.11**	−.14***	−.12**
	(.02)	(.02)	(.02)	(.03)	(.03)	(.03)	(.05)	(.04)	(.05)
Soph. remedial course	−.83*	−.78*	−.08*	1.34**	1.10*	1.22*	−2.04***	−1.69***	−1.84***
	(.46)	(.42)	(.47)	(.66)	(.64)	(.68)	(.65)	(.57)	(.67)
Soph. advanced course	1.48***	1.49***	1.47**	1.72***	1.96***	1.68***	.96	.83	1.14
	(.57)	(.56)	(.58)	(.58)	(.56)	(.59)	(1.40)	(1.36)	(1.41)
SES	.38	.43**	.36	.31	.27	.22	.48	.66**	.57
	(.23)	(.21)	(.23)	(.28)	(.26)	(.29)	(.37)	(.34)	(.37)
No. of semesters of math taken	.65***	.61***	.63***	.62**	.66***	.73**	.74**	.62***	.62
	(.23)	(.14)	(.24)	(.29)	(.18)	(.30)	(.38)	(.23)	(.38)
Student-specific set									
Mean life science prep.	−.03		−.04	−.05		−.06	−.02		−.01
	(.03)		(.04)	(.04)		(.05)	(.05)		(.06)
Mean physical science prep.	−.00		−.03	.04		.01	−.06		−.09
	(.03)		(.04)	(.04)		(.04)	(.06)		(.06)
Std. dev. of life science prep.	.06		.06	.12*		.10	−.01		−.00
	(.06)		(.06)	(.07)		(.07)	(.09)		(.10)

Std. dev. of phys. science prep.	.01 (.06)		.00 (.07)	−.05 (.07)		−.07 (.08)	.07 (.11)		.08 (.11)
No. of teachers	.12 (.39)		.12 (.39)	.48 (.51)		.39 (.52)	−.08 (.59)		.12 (.60)
School-level set									
Mean life science prep.		−.04 (.07)	.01 (.08)		−.15* (.08)	−.01 (.10)		.08 (.12)	.04 (.14)
Mean physical science prep.		.06 (.07)	.14* (.08)		−.00 (.09)	.00 (.10)		.11 (.11)	.26* (.13)
Std. dev. of life science prep.		.05 (.08)	.01 (.09)		.24*** (.09)	.17 (.10)		−.17 (.13)	−.19 (.15)
Std. dev. of physical science prep.		−.03 (.08)	−.07 (.09)		.02 (.10)	.07 (.11)		−.12 (.13)	−.25* (.14)
No. of teachers		.04 (.03)	.03 (.03)		.02 (.04)	.04 (.04)		.04 (.05)	.01 (.06)
N	1,819	2,100	1,819	977	1,090	977	842	1,010	842
R²	.06	.06	.06	.05	.05	.05	.02	.02	.02

Note: Figures in parentheses represent standard errors.

[a] ≥ median, 56.84

[b] < median, 56.84

*p < .10   **p < .05   ***p < .01

classroom or school and grade level to understand more about the complex ways in which instructional resources interact in the context of schooling organizations.

We have also sought to test our ideas empirically using survey data that permit a focus on the subject-matter preparation of teachers. Our empirical analyses of the proximate and immediate past teachers are informative and interesting, but they fall short of resolving fundamental questions about the short-term lagged effect of teacher resources on pupil performance. In hindsight, it is not surprising that we have been unable to demonstrate strong effects of teacher subject-matter preparation at the various levels we identified. We would have much preferred data measuring more directly what teachers know about the subject(s) being taught, but this kind of information is difficult to obtain. We had to settle for self-reported information about the level of study in various areas, and this seriously limited the empirical analyses we could conduct.

We had greater success in discerning the longer-term collective effects of students' previous teachers. We are intrigued by our finding that low-pretest students' performance gains in mathematics were more sensitive to the mean level of their previous teachers' preparation level than were the high-pretest students. We are also intrigued by our finding that high-pretest students in mathematics were more adversely affected by variability in the preparation level of their teachers than were the low-pretest students. The differences across our results for mathematics and science are also intriguing. It is clear that practices and results vary significantly across these important areas of the secondary school curriculum, and more analysis of the differences is clearly warranted.

In closing, we wish to stress the importance of pursuing complementary analyses of both the formation and the utilization of collective teacher resources within schools. These analyses should include examination of the hiring and separation of teachers, as well as detailed studies of how existing teacher resources are deployed within schools. It will also be important to extend these analyses with more direct measures of the subject-matter knowledge teachers add to the instructional activities found within schools.

APPENDIX 2.1

Table 2.1A.   Means and Standard Deviations of Selected Variables

	Mathematics			Science		
	N	Mean	S.D.	N	Mean	S.D.
Student Attributes						
Soph.-gain score	2,723	2.72	5.53	2,708	4.36	6.07
Junior-gain score	2,706	.81	5.59	2,689	.81	5.96
Total-gain score	2,706	3.54	6.50	2,689	5.17	6.92
Soph. pretest	2,766	60.47	11.03	2,751	57.41	10.02
Junior pretest	2,723	62.23	11.37	2,708	61.82	10.58
Senior pretest	2,706	64.06	11.93	2,689	62.64	11.04
Dummy for soph. remedial course	2,831	.21	.41	2,830	.14	.35
Dummy for soph. advanced course	2,831	.05	.21	2,830	.11	.31
Dummy for junior remedial course	2,831	.11	.31	2,830	.09	.29
Dummy for junior advanced course	2,831	.07	.25	2,830	.09	.29
Socioeconomic status[a]	2,819	− .03	.74	2,818	− .03	.74
No. of semesters of subject taken	1,990	2.97	1.09	2,227	2.75	1.11
Individual proximate teacher attributes						
Soph. preparation[b]						
Math	2,084	12.35	6.12			
Life sciences				2,045	12.33	9.60
Physical sciences				2,045	8.11	6.87
Soph. experience	2,216	15.64	8.58	2,212	15.47	8.26
Junior preparation						
Math	1,245	13.24	6.37			
Life sciences				1,150	7.62	6.72
Physical sciences				1,150	11.59	7.22
Junior experience	1,349	16.52	8.25	1,199	16.45	9.82
Student-specific set of teachers[c]						
Mean preparation						
Math	1,990	12.44	5.45			
Life sciences				2,210	9.61	5.60
Physical sciences				2,210	9.36	5.83
Std. dev. of preparation						
Math	1,773	2.55	2.86			
Life sciences				1,873	2.69	3.64
Physical sciences				1,873	2.38	3.38
No. of teachers in set	2,073	1.67	.71	2,389	1.46	.72
School-level set of teachers						
Mean preparation						
Math	2,073	10.68	2.73			
Life sciences				2,389	8.45	2.69

Physical sciences				2,389	6.38	2.34
Std. dev. of preparation						
Math	2,073	6.87	1.94			
Life sciences				2,389	9.22	2.89
Physical sciences				2,389	6.57	2.67
No. of teachers in school	2,602	11.21	4.75	2,918	8.84	4.59

[a]This is an LSAY composite variable which ranges from −300 to 300.
[b]Teacher preparation is measured by the number of subject-specific courses taken.
[c]Set of subject-specific teachers that the student had during his or her sophomore and junior years in high school.

What to Do after High School: The Two-Year versus Four-Year College Enrollment Decision

Cecilia Elena Rouse

Clark Kerr, an architect of the California university system, termed the junior college "the great innovation of American higher education in the twentieth century."[1] His point is illustrated by the fact that between 1960 and 1980 the number of public two-year institutions grew from 332 to 869, doubling in the first ten years.[2] Enrollment of first-time students exploded during the late 1960s, reaching a peak in the early 1980s.[3] In fact, during the latter half of the 1970s and the early 1980s, over one-half of all first-time, first-year students chose to enroll in junior college.[4]

A key reason for the rise in two-year college enrollment was society's growing commitment to creating equality of opportunity in higher education during the 1960s. Educators foresaw that in the late 1960s and early 1970s the "baby boom" generation would attend college, and the existing system could not accommodate it. Community colleges could thus serve the dual purpose of allowing states to preserve the quality of the four-year institutions while not having to exclude individuals from higher education.

Community colleges have traditionally strived for equality of opportunity through low, or no, tuition. Faced with skyrocketing costs of higher education, many states have had to abandon this ideal. For example, in 1992 officials at the City University of New York announced a 20 percent increase in two-year college tuition, bringing the yearly tuition to $1,050, or almost the same as the $1,100 in the four-year colleges.[5] Since most studies on the effects of college costs on college attendance consider two-

I would like to thank Susanto Basu, David Card, Richard Freeman, Alan Krueger, and Vijaya Ramachandran for useful discussions; members of the Harvard Labor lunch and seminar, and the Contemporary Policy Issues in Education conference for comments; Tom Kane for helpful suggestions and for data; and especially to Gary Chamberlain, Claudia Goldin, and Larry Katz for help and guidance. All remaining errors are my own.

year and four-year colleges together, we know little about the effects of
tuition changes on the decision to attend two-year, rather than four-
year, colleges.

Two important issues are the extent to which the attractively low
tuition and geographical convenience of community colleges divert students from four-year colleges (diversion) and to what extent they provide
a place in higher education for those who would not otherwise attend
college (democratization). Although the social importance of these issues
depends on the extent to which the type of institution in which one
begins college matters for future success—an issue that is receiving
growing attention—there have been few previous attempts to look at how
changes in higher education policy affect the composition of college enrollments.[6]

In this paper, I use the National Longitudinal Survey, Youth Cohort
(NLSY), the High School and Beyond (HSB) survey, and the October
educational supplement of the Current Population Survey (CPS) to
investigate who attends junior college, the economic motives for attending junior college, and the effects of college tuition and proximity on the
decision to attend two- and four-year college. I use a multinomial logit
(MNL) model representing three choices: starting in two-year college,
starting in four-year college, or not attending college. I find that those
students who begin in a junior college, compared to those who begin in a
four-year college, are more likely to be among the first generation in
their family to attend college; that they are more likely to be nonblack,
ceteris paribus, and to have lower levels of measured academic ability;
and that junior college enrollments appear to be more sensitive to
changes in tuition than are four-year college enrollments. I estimate that
at all levels of tuition, increases in two-year tuition primarily discourage
students from attending college altogether. For all distances, increasing
two-year college proximity equally encourages new college students and
diverts students from four-year colleges. The evidence from the CPS
generally supports the importance of relative tuition in determining
college enrollment composition, although it also suggests caution in
interpreting state variation in college tuition as a "natural experiment."

In the next section, I sketch the basic random utility framework for
modeling college choice behavior. In the third, I explain the data; and,
in the fourth, I review some of the descriptive statistics on who attends
community college. The main results are then presented in the two
following sections, and, finally, I present my conclusions.

A SKETCH OF THE FRAMEWORK

I follow many before me in modeling college choice using a random utility model in which decisions can be only probabilistically estimated. If an individual chooses one of three alternatives—no college (NC), two-year or junior college (JC), or four-year or senior college (SC) —then her utilities can be represented as

$$
\begin{aligned}
U_{i,NC} &= \overline{U}_{i,NC} + \epsilon_{i,NC} \\
U_{i,JC} &= \underline{U}_{i,JC} + \epsilon_{i,JC} \\
U_{i,SC} &= \overline{U}_{i,SC} + \epsilon_{i,SC}
\end{aligned}
\tag{3.1}
$$

where $\epsilon_{i,j}$ represents random error. An individual, i, receives utility from each alternative, j, such that

$$
U_{ij} = \beta_{ij}X_i + \delta_j T_{ij} + \epsilon_{ij}
\tag{3.2}
$$

where X represents a matrix of individual-specific characteristics, such as socioeconomic status and measured ability, and T_j represents alternative-specific characteristics, such as college tuition. An individual will choose an alternative if it maximizes her utility. That is, she chooses to start at junior college if: $U(JC)_i > U(SC)_i$ and $U(JC)_i > U(NC)_i$. The probability that she starts at junior college is thus:

$$
\begin{aligned}
Pr(U_{ijC} > U_{iSC},\ U_{ijC} > U_{iNC}) = Pr(\epsilon_{iSC} - \epsilon_{ijC} < \overline{U}_{ijC} - \overline{U}_{iSC} \\
\text{and } \epsilon_{iNC} - \epsilon_{ijC} < \overline{U}_{ijC} - \overline{U}_{iNC}).
\end{aligned}
\tag{3.3}
$$

Letting $\eta_{kk'} \equiv \epsilon_k - \epsilon_{k'}$ and $\overline{U}_{kk'} \equiv \overline{U}_k - \overline{U}_{k'}$ (and dropping the i subscript for simplicity),

$$
P_{JC} = \int_{-\infty}^{\overline{U}_{JC,SC}} \int_{-\infty}^{\overline{U}_{JC,NC}} g_{JC}(\eta_{JC,SC},\ \eta_{JC,NC}) d\eta_{JC,SC} d\eta_{JC,NC}
\tag{3.4}
$$

where g_{JC} is the joint density function of the differenced variables for the junior college alternative. The specification of the distribution of the error terms leads to different methods for estimating the model.

A MULTINOMIAL LOGIT (MNL)

The MNL assumes that the errors (ϵ's) in equation 3.1 are logistically distributed. Thus:

$$
Pr(JC)_i = \frac{\exp(\beta_{JC}X_i + \delta_j T_{JC})}{\exp \sum\limits_{j=1}^{3} (\beta_j X_i + \delta_j T_{ij})}.
\tag{3.5}
$$

Note that I allow the effects of individual-specific characteristics to differ for each choice, while I constrain alternative-specific characteristics to have an impact on only the utility for that choice.[7] Thus, two-year college tuition directly affects the individual's utility for two-year college, but it only indirectly affects her utility for four-year college. The alternative-specific coefficients may differ to the extent that I have not controlled for other characteristics of the alternatives, such as school quality.[8]

THE ASSUMPTIONS

When deciding whether or not to attend college, each student, I assume, weighs the tuition of public comprehensive four-year colleges and that of public two-year colleges in the state in which she resides. I do not believe this assumption is restrictive for two reasons. First, 81 percent of all new ("new" to the reporting institution) undergraduate students are residents of the state in which they are enrolled in school, a percentage that is certainly higher for community college students.[9] Second, 65 percent of first-time, first-year, four-year college students and 90 percent of first-time, first-year, two-year college students are in public institutions.[10] Thus, the average student attends a public institution in her state of residence.

I also assume that all three options are part of every student's opportunity set, even though it is unlikely that all students who choose to attend junior college would have been admitted by a four-year college. Similarly, while it makes intuitive sense that students considering junior college would more likely weigh this option against a public comprehensive college, as opposed to an elite, private university, some students might consider a four-year college only if it is of a significantly higher perceived quality than the community college under consideration. These students might think that the local junior college is fairly similar to a four-year comprehensive college in quality and is less expensive. If they are going to attend a four-year institution, they will attend a significantly more expensive four-year university. Without explicitly modeling college application and acceptance, however, I believe that the assumption is fairly innocuous.

Tuition is the only cost included in the estimations. Since many two-year college students live at home, this measure is close to the actual cost for them.[11] However, tuition alone underestimates the total cost for four-year students. If room and board are an omitted variable positively correlated with four-year college tuition and negatively correlated with four-year college choice, I should overestimate the price sensitivity of four-year enrollments. Another element of cost I have omitted is financial aid. Aside from using information on applications and admissions (which would be particularly difficult since many community colleges have no formal application process) and the financial aid offered by specific institutions, there is little data on expected financial aid. Kane (1991) simulates Pell Grant eligibility and finds a small positive effect on enrollments. However, once he controls for family income, tuition, and time effects, there is little variability left in the Pell Grant eligibility rules. He finds that while financial aid is important, changes in tuition are more important. Manski and Wise (1983) use the National Longitudinal Study of the High School Class of 1972 (NLS72), a survey of high school seniors in 1972, to simulate the effects of federal aid (the Basic Educational Opportunity Grant [BEOG] program) on college enrollment. They conclude that financial aid affects the decision to attend two-year, but not four-year, college. In fact, they believe that the entire increase in two-year enrollments during the 1970s can be attributed to increases in financial aid. However, since BEOG grants were not initiated until 1973, it is unclear how much information the students actually had about the program while they were high school seniors.

Finally, to identify the importance of tuition and college proximity in the decision as to which kind of college to attend, I rely on the fact that states differ in their higher education policy. For example, nearly 66 percent of California's college enrollment is in two-year colleges, compared to 25 percent for Massachusetts and 5 percent for Wyoming.[12] Similarly, states vary in their tuition rates. Rhode Island—which has a lone public two-year college—charged a total of $1,004 for tuition, fees, and room and board in 1989, compared to California, which charged only $112.[13] While the variation in state policy provides a natural experiment with which to study college investment decisions, there is some concern that whether a student attends a two-year college or an open-door, four-year college is less a matter of individual decision making and more a question of institutional labeling. Admissions standards and course content in one state's community colleges may be the same as in another state's four-year colleges. To control for some state effects, I include the number of two-year schools and four-year schools per capita (of those eighteen to twenty-four years old), the real income per capita (in 1982 dollars), direct general state expenditure on education per capita (in 1982 dollars), and manufacturing employment as a share of total civilian employment.[14]

DATA

THE NATIONAL LONGITUDINAL SURVEY, YOUTH COHORT

The NLSY is a national longitudinal survey with a base sample of 12,868 people aged fourteen to twenty-two when they were first surveyed in 1979. The participants have been resurveyed every year since and have been asked detailed questions about their educational, work, and personal experiences. I assume that survey participants made decisions based on their state of residence, tuition, and family income when they were eighteen years old. I thus assume that the individuals made decisions from 1978 to 1983, during the peak of first-time, first-year enrollments in two-year colleges. I then determine whether the subjects have attended college and classify the first college they report having attended as either a two- or a four-year school.[15]

I consider only those who have completed at least twelve years of education, since four-year schools are not an option for high school dropouts.[16] Pincus (1980) argues that looking at only high school graduates underestimates the class and race differences in college attendance because minorities and those from lower-income families are more likely to drop out of high school.[17] However, Cameron and Heckman (1992) find that jointly estimating previous education decisions, such as high school graduation, and college enrollment does not explain racial differences in college attendance but does increase the importance of labor market variables on educational attainment.

I estimate the model defining college attendance for those who first attended between the ages of seventeen and nineteen, although, in my sample, some individuals began college at age twenty-eight.[18] Of all those in the NLSY who attended junior college, about 81 percent did so by the age of twenty; of all those who attended four-year college, 91 percent did so by the same age. The disparity clearly arises from the mission of the junior college to allow for delayed entry. I also use net family income (in 1982 dollars) and number of children in the family to control for a family's ability to pay. The mother's and the father's years of education are used as a proxy for socioeconomic status, as is the respondent's possible information about, and value attached to, college.

An AFQT score—a linear combination of the arithmetic reasoning, word knowledge, paragraph completion, and numerical operation tests from the military's ASVAB battery of skills—measures ability. The asset of this proxy is that almost all of the survey participants took the test; however, it was administered to them in different years and at different stages of their education. The measure likely embodies a mixture of "innate ability" (in the bookish sense) and prior educational experiences.[19]

The primary sample includes 3,645 individuals; means and standard deviations are reported in Table 3.1A in the appendix to this chapter. While relatively small, the NLSY sample has the advantage over the October CPS of including measures of ability, better measures of family background, and indicating the first college attended. The advantage over the HSB is that the NLSY includes different cohorts.

HIGH SCHOOL AND BEYOND

The HSB is a national longitudinal survey following 11,995 high school seniors from 1,015 different schools in 1980. The survey participants were resurveyed in 1982, 1984, and 1986, with about 88 percent of the sample still participating in the last wave. As with the NLSY, I classify individuals according to the type of college first attended after high school; their opportunity sets are based upon their state of residence while seniors in high school. Although the HSB has the disadvantage that the variation in tuition is solely cross-sectional, it has the advantage that it includes an additional policy instrument: The high school counselors were asked the number of miles from the students' high school to the nearest two-year and four-year colleges, which provides a measure of college availability. In addition, all of the participants were administered a battery of ability tests at the same stage of their education, during the spring of their senior year in high school. Sample means and standard deviations are in the appendix (Table 3.2A).

OCTOBER CURRENT POPULATION SURVEY

The October CPS includes a supplement about the education of those currently enrolled in school. The questions include current year in school, type of school, and control of school. Hence, for those aged eighteen to nineteen, I record whether they are enrolled in college and whether it is a two- or a four-year college. Because only current enrollment is reported, I do not know whether these are truly the first colleges attended. Nonetheless, the enrollment rates are similar to those reported in the NLSY. From the CPS, I take only those who are not heads of households and who have at least twelve years of education. I also record gender, race (black or nonblack), mother's and father's education (actually, the education of the heads of household), family income (in 1982 dollars), and central city status. Although I present state-level estimates, the results are quite similar using the individual data. (See the appendix, Table 3.3A, for sample means and standard deviations.)

LABOR MARKET VARIABLES

A local unemployment rate in the NLSY, the county unemployment rate in the HSB, and the state unemployment rate in the CPS measure the opportunity cost of attending college.[20] As indicators of expected returns to each alternative, two measures are tested. First, I use an average wage of persons aged twenty-four to fifty-four with a high school degree, with "some" college (thirteen to fifteen years of education), and with four years of college in the state of residence and in the relevant year. I also use an experience-adjusted wage differential that varies by education, race, gender, region, and year.[21] Note that I implicitly assume the students have myopic expectations as they respond to the existing wage differentials without an attempt to anticipate future demand and supply conditions. Conceivably, one could experiment with different models of expectations of returns to education, allowing for more information on the part of the students. In addition, a more conceptually correct return would be the return to college for those who attended college in the respondent's state, a correction that requires more information about individuals than is readily available.

The tuition data are collected from the Washington State Board of Higher Education and represent a state average of the in-state tuition and fees at public comprehensive universities and community colleges. Although the four-year tuition data are available beginning in 1972, the two-year data run from 1978 to 1988.

WHO GOES TO JUNIOR COLLEGE? THE DESCRIPTIVE STATISTICS

College attendance patterns among participants in the NLSY and the HSB are shown in Table 3.1. With few exceptions, the two surveys estimate similar college attendance patterns.[22] Overall about 30 percent of female high school graduates will attend junior college at some point, representing at least one-half of those who ever attend college. About 40

Table 3.1. College Attendance Patterns: NLSY vs. HSB (Weighted)

Women

	Conditional on 12 yrs. Education		Conditional on Attending College	
	NLSY	HSB	NLSY	HSB
% Ever attend college	63.7	61.2		
% Ever attend JC	36.8	30.1	57.7	49.3
% Ever attend four-yr.	42.5	43.3	66.6	70.8
% Attend only JC	21.2	18.9	33.3	29.2
% Attend only four-yr.	26.9	32.6	42.3	50.7
% Attend both	15.5	12.6	24.4	20.1
% 1st college = JC			45.4	39.0
No. of observations	2,925	3,861	1,815	2,446

Men

	Conditional on 12 yrs. Education		Conditional on Attending College	
	NLSY	HSB	NLSY	HSB
% Ever attend college	60.2	60.4		
% Ever attend JC	31.1	28.3	51.5	46.8
% Ever attend four-yr.	44.4	45.8	73.7	75.8
% Attend only JC	15.9	15.4	26.3	24.2
% Attend only four-yr.	29.2	33.9	48.4	53.2
% Attend both	15.2	13.8	25.2	22.5
% 1st college = JC			40.5	37.4
No. of observations	2,802	3,024	1,614	1,906

Blacks

	Conditional on 12 yrs. Education		Conditional on Attending College	
	NLSY	HSB	NLSY	HSB
% Ever attend college	58.3	56.6		
% Ever attend JC	32.3	26.3	55.4	46.5
% Ever attend four-yr.	38.5	40.4	66.1	71.3
% Attend only JC	19.8	17.2	33.9	28.7
% Attend only four-yr.	26.0	31.6	44.6	53.5
% Attend both	12.5	10.4	21.5	17.9
% 1st college = JC			43.1	34.9
No. of observations	1,306	1,492	752	865

Nonblacks

	Conditional on 12 yrs. Education		Conditional on Attending College	
	NLSY	HSB	NLSY	HSB
% Ever attend college	62.4	61.3		
% Ever attend JC	34.1	29.6	54.7	48.3
% Ever attend four-yr.	44.0	44.8	70.5	73.2
% Attend only JC	18.4	17.4	29.5	26.8
% Attend only four-yr.	28.3	33.3	45.3	51.7
% Attend both	15.7	13.4	25.2	21.5
% 1st college = JC			43.0	38.6
No. of observations	4,421	5,393	2,677	3,487

percent of women who attend college begin in a junior college. Men, on the other hand, make slightly less use of these neighborhood institutions. The differences between blacks and nonblacks are small, although these estimates may underestimate regional variation in the importance of junior college for blacks due to the fact that in the south there are many predominately black four-year institutions.

Table 3.2 profiles the individuals by their choice of postsecondary activity. The two-year college population is disproportionately female; and while blacks are slightly overrepresented among those who choose not to go to college, their proportions in the two types of colleges mirror their numbers in the overall population. The family incomes, the parents' education, and the AFQT scores of those attending two-year college suggest that junior college is a middle ground between no college and four-year college. One exception is the family income for blacks who attend four-year college, which is about 22 percent higher than that for those who attend two-year college, compared with a 14 percent difference between two-year students and those who do not attend college. Sixty-eight percent of those who first attend junior college in general and 75 percent of those who first enroll between the ages of seventeen and nineteen attend full-time.

Who Goes to Community College? MNL Results

THE NATIONAL LONGITUDINAL SURVEY, YOUTH COHORT

The Importance of Socioeconomics, Race, and Measured Ability. Table 3.3 presents multinomial logit results of the choice of postsecondary activity that highlight the effects of socioeconomic variables, race, and measured ability using the NLSY. The columns represent estimates with and without controls for region effects or state variables that might be correlated with college attendance and tuition.

On the whole, the results of other researchers are confirmed.[23] Race, measured ability, and socioeconomic status distinguish those who attend college from those who do not. Conditional on family income, women are more likely than men, and blacks are far more likely than nonblacks, to attend college. While women are equally likely to attend the two types of institutions, blacks tend toward four-year college. The better educated one's parents are, the more family resources are available (as measured by family income and family size), and the greater one's measured ability is, the more likely one is to attend college. In addition, the higher the

Table 3.2. Demographics of Postsecondary School Choice

	All			Black			Nonblack		
	No College	Two-year College	Four-year College	No College	Two-year College	Four-year College	No College	Two-year College	Four-year College
Female	49.2	53.9	48.6	46.3	63.8	55.7	49.7	52.9	47.8
Black	12.4	9.6	10.2						
AFQT[a]	66.6	75.9	85.3	47.6	56.2	67.5	69.3	78.0	87.3
Family income[b]	23,538	28,724	33,569	15,941	18,876	22,044	24,614	29,774	34,875
Mother's education[c]	11.1	12.1	13.0	10.8	11.3	12.2	11.2	12.1	13.1
Father's education[c]	11.0	12.4	13.8	10.0	10.6	11.8	11.1	12.6	14.0
No. of siblings	3.4	3.0	3.7	4.8	4.1	3.6	3.2	2.9	2.6
Northeast	21.0	19.3	23.7	21.0	19.6	21.3	21.0	19.3	24.0
Northcentral	35.2	27.5	34.4	20.5	18.3	20.2	37.3	28.5	36.0
South	27.0	28.7	30.2	52.5	47.1	54.1	23.4	26.7	27.5
West	16.8	24.5	11.7	5.9	15.0	4.3	18.3	25.5	12.5
Central city	14.4	12.8	18.4	33.3	35.7	38.9	11.8	10.4	16.1
Attend full-time		75.9	92.9		83.3	94.6		75.2	92.7
No. of observations	2,923	1,128	1,676	707	234	365	2,216	894	1,311

Note: Figures represent percentage of the column heading unless otherwise noted. Region and family income are for 18-year-old respondents. Region refers to area of residence in the United States.

[a]Raw score.
[b]In 1982 dollars
[c]In years.

Table 3.3. MNL Estimates of Postsecondary Activity: NLSY

Independent Variables	log [Pr (2 yr.)/ Pr (No Coll.)]	log [Pr (4 yr.)/ Pr (No Coll.)]	Add Region Dummies		Add State/Time Variables	
			log [Pr (2 yr.)/ Pr (No Coll.)]	log [Pr (4 yr.)/ Pr (No Coll.)]	log [Pr (2 yr.)/ Pr (No Coll.)]	log [Pr (4 yr.)/ Pr (No Coll.)]
Family income[a]	0.1291 (0.0311)	0.1720 (0.0304)	0.0673 (0.0321)	0.1259 (0.0325)	0.1056 (0.0318)	0.1814 (0.0312)
Female	0.2873 (0.0920)	0.2865 (0.0941)	0.4073 (0.0904)	0.3929 (0.0967)	0.2790 (0.0934)	0.2821 (0.0953)
Black	0.7503 (0.1285)	1.6751 (0.1305)	0.9570 (0.1279)	1.6761 (0.1382)	0.8497 (0.1338)	1.6389 (0.1368)
Mother HS grad. *	0.3973 (0.1138)	0.4444 (0.1224)	0.2944 (0.1082)	0.3822 (0.1203)	0.4439 (0.1158)	0.4616 (0.1240)
Mother some college	0.5358 (0.1717)	0.6560 (0.1760)	0.7277 (0.1825)	1.0230 (0.1893)	0.5479 (0.1732)	0.7038 (0.1781)
Mother college grad.	0.4965 (0.2280)	0.8790 (0.2051)	0.7719 (0.2729)	1.3546 (0.2632)	0.5029 (0.2306)	0.8865 (0.2083)
Father HS grad. *	0.2069 (0.1127)	−0.0213 (0.1225)	0.2192 (0.1067)	0.0699 (0.1201)	0.1548 (0.1144)	0.0010 (0.1241)
Father some college	0.4601 (0.1665)	0.5803 (0.1686)	0.5482 (0.1673)	0.6579 (0.1737)	0.3929 (0.1701)	0.6010 (0.1706)
Father college grad.	0.7441 (0.1772)	1.1642 (0.1756)	1.0989 (0.1988)	1.4843 (0.2055)	0.6577 (0.1803)	1.1700 (0.1777)

Variable	Model 1 (no/no)		Model 2 (yes/no)		Model 3 (no/yes)	
Log of family size	−0.5018 (0.1390)	−0.6141 (0.1397)	−0.4994 (0.1363)	−0.5696 (0.1462)	−0.5212 (0.1419)	−0.5926 (0.1424)
AFQT[b]	0.2853 (0.0301)	0.6733 (0.0331)	0.3443 (0.0300)	0.7111 (0.0334)	0.3000 (0.0314)	0.6851 (0.0338)
Unemployment rate	0.0497 (0.0132)	0.0321 (0.0142)	0.0307 (0.0133)	0.0303 (0.1478)	0.0636 (0.1870)	0.0090 (0.0194)
Central city status	0.1466 (0.1233)	0.4095 (0.1180)	0.0515 (0.1227)	0.4298 (0.1250)	0.0948 (0.1279)	0.4553 (0.1228)
Two-year tuition[c]	−1.4858 (0.1506)		−1.1497 (0.2345)		−0.6795 (0.2091)	
Four-year tuition[c]		−0.5714 (0.1429)		−0.5305 (0.2048)		−0.3502 (0.1739)
Region/Time	no/no		yes/no		no/yes	
State variables	no		no		yes	
−2*log-likelihood	6,223.5		6,454.9		6,097.6	

Note: Dependent variable: 0 = no college; 1 = two-year college; 2 = four-year college. Figures in parentheses represent asymptotic standard errors. N = 3,645: no college = 1,819; two-year college = 784; four-year college = 1,042. The equations also include a constant.

*Base group consists of parents who have not completed high school.

[a] In 1982 dollars, coefficient multiplied by 10,000.

[b] Raw score, coefficient multiplied by 10.

[c] In 1982 dollars, coefficient multiplied by 1,000.

unemployment rate is, the more likely it is that individuals will attend both types of colleges. Race, parents' socioeconomic status, and measured ability also distinguish the choice of two-year and four-year school, with the addition that those living in central cities are much more likely to attend four-year schools. [24]

To interpret the logit coefficients, I first predict a "base" probability for each individual using their original values for the explanatory variables. I then change the variable of interest by a specific magnitude for each individual. (Thus, to evaluate the effect of a one standard deviation increase in test score, I add one standard deviation to each individual's original score.) I calculate a new probability for each individual and report the mean difference in the probabilities. For indicator variables, I estimate a base probability assuming that each person is the indicator variable's base group, and then I assume that every person is the other group. Again, I report the mean difference in the individual probabilities.

Predicted probabilities from the coefficients in columns 1 and 3 of Table 3.3 are reported in Table 3.4 whether or not the estimates are significantly different from zero. Conditional on family income, we see a difference of 0.28 in the probability of starting in four-year college between those whose parents both graduated from college and those whose parents did not finish high school. That these factors significantly differ for two-year and four-year college is robust to the many specifications I tried as well. The fact that parents' education is such an important determinant of college attendance has several interpretations. First, students of college-educated parents may have much better information about the costs and expected benefits of college, and these families may be more willing to make the human capital investment. (This would also suggest that better information about college would be an important policy goal to attract those students who are likely to succeed in college but who know little about it.) On the other hand, parents' education may be a better proxy for permanent income than is current family income. We can interpret the result that parents' education is less important for two-year college entrance as evidence that junior colleges do provide equality of opportunity. However, ability to pay is still instrumental to four-year college entrance.

A one standard deviation increase in AFQT score increases the probability that a student will begin college in a four-year school by about 0.19, ceteris paribus. While measured ability embodies a combination of nature and nurture, it most likely serves as an indicator of an individual's preparedness for college. Conditional on measured ability, and to some extent on family background, there is a difference of 0.2 in the likelihood

Table 3.4. Changes in Probability of Attending Two- or Four-Year College: NLSY

| | Change in Probability of College Attendance | | | |
| | (1) | | (3) | |
Independent Variable	Two-Year	Four-Year	Two-Year w/State Variables	Four-Year w/State Variables
$100[a] increase in tuition				
Two-year	−2.4	+0.9	−1.0	+0.4
Four-year	+0.4	−0.9	+0.2	−0.5
Both	−1.9	+0.04	−0.8	−0.1
8% increase in tuition				
Two-year	−0.9	+0.4	−0.4	+0.2
Four-year	+0.2	−0.6	+0.1	−0.4
Both	−0.7	−0.3	−0.3	−0.2
$1,000[a] increase in family income	+0.1	+0.2	+0.1	+0.2
1% decrease in unemployment	−0.1	0.0	−0.9	+0.2
Increase in parents' education*				
Both parents are HS graduates	+7.5	+3.1	+7.0	+3.7
Both parents have some college	+8.4	+14.2	+6.9	+15.6
Both parents are college graduates	+5.0	+27.6	+3.9	+28.1
Black vs. nonblack	−0.5	+21.7	+1.5	+19.9
Women vs. men	+2.8	+2.5	+2.6	+2.5
Increase AFQT by 1 St.d.	0.0	+18.5	−0.2	+18.5
Decrease family member by 1	+4.0	+6.2	+4.4	+5.7
Lives in central city	−0.4	+5.5	−1.4	+6.5

Note: The probabilities are evaluated using the individual data. (See text for an explanation.) The estimates are from Table 3.3, the first and third models.
*The parents' education is compared to both parents not having graduated from high school.
[a]In 1982 dollars.

that blacks and nonblacks will begin in a four-year college. Manski and Wise (1983) find a similar result in the NLS72 and attribute it to the fact that blacks are more likely to attend school in the south where there are many predominately black four-year schools. However, the evidence here suggests that this is but a very small part of the explanation. Instead, it appears that either the tests are a poorer proxy for blacks' ability than they are for nonblacks, or colleges use different criteria for selecting minorities ("race-norming"), or both. Even if blacks and other minorities are overrepresented in junior colleges, this can be explained by their socioeconomic status and academic preparedness for college, rather than by their race per se. Overall, the effects of measured ability and socioeconomic status indicate that junior colleges provide a place in higher education for those who cannot continue their education in a four-year college because of inadequate resources, information, or academic preparation.

What about Price? The Investment Motive. The overall change that I estimate in the decision to attend college in response to changes in tuition are similar to those estimated by others.[25] I estimate that a $100 increase in both two-year and four-year tuition decreases the likelihood of enrollment by 1.3. Leslie and Brinkman's (1988) meta-analysis of the literature on the impact of tuition on college enrollment concludes that $100 increase in tuition (in 1982 dollars) will lead to a 0.7–0.9 decrease in probability in college enrollment rates for high school graduates. Similarly, Kane (1991) estimates that a similar increase results in a change of –0.5 in the likelihood of college attendance for blacks. One difficulty with comparing these price effects with those reported by Leslie and Brinkman is that their $100 increase was based on an average college cost (including tuition and room and board) of $3,420. The average four-year tuition in this study is about $900, and the average two-year tuition is about $500 (both in 1982–83 dollars). Hence, I report the expected change in enrollment for a similar percentage increase in price of about 8 percent as well as an increase of $100. An 8 percent increase in two-year and four-year tuition decreases the overall probability of enrollment by 1.0.

The results, without additional state variables but accounting for measured ability, indicate that an 8 percent increase in two-year tuition will decrease the probability of college enrollment by 0.7, with the probability of enrolling in a two-year school decreasing 0.9 and the likelihood of attending four-year college increasing 0.2. An 8 percent increase in four-year tuition will decrease the probability of enrolling in college by 0.2, with the probability of two-year enrollment increasing 0.4 and four-year enrollment dropping 0.6. If both tuition rates rise simultaneously, there is an overall predicted drop in enrollment of 1.0, with about 70 percent of it accounted for by changes in two-year enroll-ment. When the other state controls are included, the price responses decrease: An 8 percent increase in tuition generates a decline of –0.5 percent in overall college enrollments equally shared by the two types of colleges, a similar result to that found in previous studies.

Conditional on other factors, parents' income is not a crucial determi-nant of college attendance. And in results not shown here, I find that responsiveness to tuition does not vary significantly by income, a finding in contrast to that found by previous researchers. Using the School to

College: Opportunities for Postsecondary Education (SCOPE) survey—a longitudinal survey of high school seniors in 1966 in California, Illinois, Massachusetts, and North Carolina—Kohn, Manski, and Mundel (1976) model the choice set, as well as the choice of institution, and conclude that students from higher-income families are less sensitive to price (including both tuition and room and board costs) and that parental education is less important in families with higher incomes.[26] Mismeasurement of income in the NLSY may explain the weak effect of family income.

While the differential impacts of family background and measured ability are robust to different specifications, the effects of tuition are less stable. Nonetheless, in most specifications, two-year enrollments respond more to price than do four-year enrollments. The exception is when other state variables are included. The two-year own-price effect drops in magnitude but remains statistically significant; the four-year own-price effect is barely significantly different from zero. In fact, the only price variable that remained significant throughout all of the trials (of those that did not employ state dummies) was the two-year own-price. Although this mixed evidence calls for caution in interpretation, there are reasons to believe that changes in college tuition primarily affect two-year college attendance.

Costs and Benefits: Evidence from the NLSY. Given that the previous logits did not include returns to education, the greater price responsiveness of two-year students may reflect omitted variables, such as college quality or returns to education. Table 3.5 displays the coefficients from MNLs using a subset of the NLSY—those who were eighteen years old between 1979 and 1983—to include the measures of returns to education estimated using the CPS. Because the socioeconomic and demographic estimates did not change significantly, I do not present them; instead, I focus on the investment motive for attending college. The upper panel of the table has four columns, each representing different ways to measure returns to education. The first three are based on a log-wage regression, and the fourth represents average wages of workers in each state in each year (as discussed above). This panel shows that tuition is still significantly related to college choice, even after controlling for estimated returns. In addition, two-year college enrollment remains more sensitive to tuition than does four-year college enrollment. (Remember that two-year tuition directly affects only the utility one receives from attending two-year college, as do the returns.) Similarly, in specifications 1 and 3, students appear to positively respond to expected returns, both for two-year

Table 3.5. *Responsiveness to Costs and Benefits in Choice of Postsecondary*
School (MNL Estimates: NLSY, 1979–83)

	Estimated Returns to Education			Average Earnings by Education Group
Cost Variables	(1)	(2)	(3)	(4)
Two-year tuition[a]	−0.7556	−0.7017	−0.0882	−0.7322
	(0.2246)	(0.2236)	(0.0237)	(0.2229)
Four-year tuition[a]	−0.4269	−0.4375	−0.0459	−0.4207
	(0.1833)	(0.1837)	(0.0184)	(0.1835)
Return to some college[b]	6.0422	−4.9952	8.3619	−12.00
	(2.3535)	(6.1478)	(3.2933)	(11.26)
Return to college[b]	2.0821	4.2442	4.9116	−17.16
	(1.2141)	(2.1287)	(1.5713)	(8.99)
−2* log-likelihood	5234.4	5237.6	5229.6	5238.6

Change in Probability of College Attendance

	Specification (1)		Specification (3)	
Cost Variables	Two-Year	Four-Year	Two-Year	Four-Year
Increase tuition by $2,600				
Two-year tuition[c]	−0.37	+0.14	−0.41	+0.16
Four-year tuition[c]	0.07	−0.19	0.08	−0.19
Increase return by 0.5%				
Some college	+0.53	−0.20	+0.75	−0.29
College	−0.07	+0.16	−0.17	+0.39

Note: Dependent variable: 0 = no college; 1 = two-year college; 2 = four-year college.
Figures in parentheses represent asymtotic standard errors. The specifications are: (1)
returns vary by time, region, gender, and race; (2) returns vary by time, gender, and race;
(3) returns vary by time, region, and gender; (4) state average wages by education group
over time. (See text for an explanation of how the returns were computed.) $N = 3,075$: no
college = 1,521; two-year college = 675; four-year college = 879. Other variables included
were: a constant; parents' income; female, black; mother's and father's education; family
size; AFQT score; central city status; unemployment rate; number of two-year and four-
year schools per capita by state; real state expenditures on education; real income per
capita; and percent employed in manufacturing.

[a] In 1982 dollars, coefficient multiplied by 1,000.
[b] Relative to high school graduate.
[c] Coefficient multiplied by 1,000.

and four-year college. The coefficients are positive and significant, and
potential two-year students appear to pay slightly more attention to
their anticipated rewards from attending college. The coefficients in
specifications 2 and 4 are either negative or insignificant. Since the
returns in specification 2 vary only by gender, race, and year, and those

in specification 4 only by state and year, I believe that the estimates result from insufficient variation in the returns.

In the lower panel, I compare the change in probability for an expected increase of $2,600 in college tuition and an increase of 0.5 percent in the college returns.[27] In specification 1, a $2,600 increase in two-year college tuition is associated with a decrease of 0.37 in the likelihood that an individual will elect to attend a two-year college. A similar increase in lifetime earnings will increase the probability that an individual will start at a junior college by 0.53. The changes are of similar magnitude and opposite in sign. In addition, the two-year enrollments are more sensitive to the own-return to "some college."

The criticism that students attend two-year institutions even though they would benefit more from a four-year college can be restated as, When students enroll in junior college they are responding to economic returns to four years of college. I find, however, that individuals make "rational" decisions and respond to both types of returns. Nonetheless, it appears that increases in the payoff to "some college" decrease four-year enrollments more than similar increases in the return to four-year college decrease two-year enrollments. I also tried estimating these equations separately for blacks and nonblacks, men and women, individuals from low-income and high-income families, and individuals with low and high test scores. The results, although tentative (due to large standard errors rather than close point estimates) and not presented here, suggest that responsiveness to tuition changes does not change with family income, race, or gender, but that those in the lowest three ability quartiles responded more to changes in two-year college tuition than did those from the upper quartile.

HIGH SCHOOL AND BEYOND: DEMOCRATIZATION OR DIVERSION? ENROLLMENT EFFECTS OF POLICY INSTRUMENTS

Table 3.6 presents an MNL using the HSB in which I include an additional cost variable: the number of miles from the respondent's high school to the nearest two-year and four-year colleges. The coefficients from the HSB on the individual characteristics closely resemble those in the NLSY.

In Tables 3.7 and 3.8, I estimate magnitudes of democratization and diversion by looking at the predicted probability of starting in a two-year or a four-year college for different levels of community college tuition and proximity. To identify the extent of democratization and diversion, I decompose the change in likelihood of attending two-year college into

Table 3.6. MNL Estimates of Postsecondary Activity: HSB

Independent Variables	log [Pr (2 yr.)/ Pr (No Coll.)]	log [Pr (4 yr.)/ Pr (No Coll.)]
Family income[a]	0.0166 (0.0258)	0.1052 (0.0246)
Female	0.2006 (0.0689)	0.3685 (0.0664)
Black	0.0337 (0.0880)	1.1034 (0.0821)
Mother* HS grad.	−0.0332 (0.0797)	−0.1084 (0.0765)
Mother some college	0.5376 (0.1227)	0.4911 (0.1151)
Mother college grad.	0.5198 (0.1439)	0.8771 (0.1306)
Father* HS grad.	0.2292 (0.0890)	0.2546 (0.0847)
Father some college	0.5350 (0.1227)	0.4777 (0.1205)
Father college grad.	0.6282 (0.1273)	0.9878 (0.1178)
Test score[b]	0.5030 (0.0441)	1.4783 (0.4472)
Unemployment rate	0.0309 (0.1201)	0.4304 (0.1247)
Urban	−0.0276 (0.0759)	0.1574 (0.0745)
Two-year tuition[c]	−1.5326 (0.1170)	
Four-year tuition[c]		−0.3131 (0.0990)
Miles to nearest two-year college[b]	−0.2056 (0.0157)	
Miles to nearest four-year college[b]		−0.0814 (0.0142)
Return to some college	2.0523 (0.7560)	
Return to college		1.9832 (0.5381)
−2*log-likelihood	13,640.2	

Note: Dependent variable: 0 = no college; 1 = two-year college; 2 = four-year college. Figures in parentheses represent asymptotic standard errors. $N = 7,746$: no college = 2,904; two-year college = 1,880; four-year college = 2,962. The equations also included a constant, missing flags for parents' income and education, and real state income per capita in 1980.
*The base group consists of parents who have not completed high school.
[a]In 1980 dollars, coefficient multiplied by 10,000.
[b]Coefficient multiplied by 10.
[c]In 1982 dollars, coefficient multiplied by 1,000.

Table 3.7. Effect of Two-Year College Tuition and Proximity on College Attendance: HSB

	Probability of Starting in a Two-Year College					
	Miles to the Nearest Two-Year College					
Two-year Tuition[a]	0	5	10	15	20	25
$0	45.4	43.0	40.6	38.3	36.0	33.7
$250	36.6	34.3	32.2	30.1	28.0	26.1
$500	28.6	26.6	24.7	22.9	21.2	19.6
$750	21.7	20.0	18.5	17.0	15.7	14.4
$900	18.1	16.7	15.3	14.1	12.9	11.8
$1,150	13.2	12.1	11.1	10.1	9.2	8.4
	Probability of Starting in a Four-Year College					
	Miles to the Nearest Two-Year College					
Two-year Tuition[a]	0	5	10	15	20	25
$0	28.1	29.3	30.5	31.6	32.7	33.8
$250	32.4	33.5	34.6	35.6	36.5	37.5
$500	36.3	37.2	38.1	39.0	39.8	40.6
$750	39.6	40.4	41.1	41.8	42.5	43.1
$900	41.3	42.0	42.6	43.2	43.8	44.3
$1,150	43.6	44.1	44.6	45.1	45.5	45.9

Note: Estimated from the coefficient estimates in Table 3.6. The predicted probabilities are estimated using the individual data. (See text for details.)
[a]In 1982 dollars.

the change in total probability of attending college (that is, $\Delta Pr[JC] + \Delta Pr[SC]$), or the movement from none to two-year or four-year college (democratization), and the residual, which I interpret as those diverted from four-year to two-year college.

The effects of moving the nearest community college closer to the respondent's high school in 5-mile increments at two levels of tuition are shown in the upper panel of Table 3.8. As the schools get closer, the likelihood that a student is diverted from a four-year college increases, but so does the likelihood that someone who was not considering college will now attend a two-year school. Nevertheless, the percentage of diverted students as a percentage of the total change in two-year college attendance remains roughly constant at 47 percent when junior colleges are moved from 25 miles to 20 miles and when schools are moved from 5 miles to 0 miles. At a higher rate of two-year college tuition, the equivalent estimates are 50 percent and 45 percent. For all of the proximity changes considered here, the proportion diverted from a four-year school is about the same as the proportion encouraged to start college.

Table 3.8. Estimates of the Effects of Changes in Community College Policy on the Probability of Enrolling in a Two-Year College

	Change Two-Year College Proximity (holding tuition constant)				
	25 → 20 Miles	20 → 15 Miles	15 → 10 Miles	10 → 5 Miles	5 → 0 Miles
Two-year college tuition = $250					
Total two-year change[a]	+1.9	+2.1	+2.1	+2.1	+2.3
Total college change[b]	+1.0	+1.2	+1.1	+1.0	+1.2
Diversion[c]	+0.9	+0.9	+1.0	+1.1	+1.1
Two-year college tuition = $500					
Total two-year change	+1.6	+1.7	+1.8	+1.9	+2.0
Total college change	+0.8	+0.9	+0.9	+1.0	+1.1
Diversion	+0.8	+0.8	+0.9	+0.9	+0.9
	Change Two-Year College Tuition (holding proximity constant)				
	$1150 → 900	$900 → 750	$750 → 500	$500 → 250	$250 → 0
Two-year college distance = 15 miles					
Total two-year change	+4.0	+2.9	+5.9	+7.2	+8.2
Total college change	+2.1	+1.5	+3.1	+3.8	+4.2
Diversion	+1.9	+1.4	+2.8	+3.4	+4.0
Two-year college distance = 5 miles					
Total two-year change	+4.6	+3.3	+6.6	+7.7	+8.7
Total college change	+2.5	+1.7	+3.4	+4.0	+4.5
Diversion	+2.1	+1.6	+3.2	+3.7	+4.2

Note: Calculated from the predicted probabilities in Table 3.7.

[a] "Total two-year change" indicates the change in probability of enrolling in a two-year school with the change in policy.

[b] "Total college change" refers to the change in probability of attending two- or four-year college.

[c] "Diversion" refers to the difference between the total change in likelihood of enrolling in college and the likelihood of enrolling in a two-year college; these changes reflect those who switched from four- to two-year college.

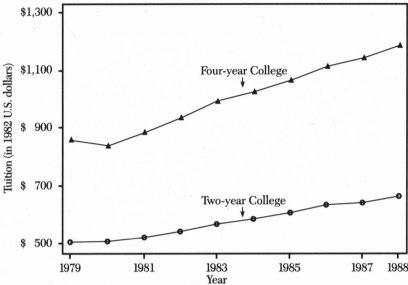

Figure 3.1. *Two-Year and Four-Year College Tuition, 1979–88*

In the bottom panel, I vary two-year tuition and hold two-year college proximity constant. At all levels of tuition, while students are diverted from four-year colleges, at an increasing rate as tuition falls, even more people are induced to go to college such that democratization outweighs diversion. Thus it appears that low community college tuition provides a better means of increasing aggregate college enrollment rates than does community college proximity.

INCREASES OVER THE 1980S: RESULTS FROM THE OCTOBER CPS

Figure 3.1 shows that throughout the 1980s college tuition increased substantially and average four-year college tuition rose slightly faster than two-year college tuition. Using the pooled sample of the 1979–88 October CPSs, I use state averages to estimate whether the change in relative tuition rates affected the two-year versus the four-year composition of college enrollments. Table 3.9 shows OLS estimates of the effect of relative two-year tuition (two-year/four-year tuition) on the diversion of four-year college students to two-year colleges (two-year/four-year enrollment) in levels. Panel A shows estimates constraining the effects to be similar for all states. Without year or geographical effects, a 1 percent increase in two-year tuition relative to four-year tuition would decrease the two-year enrollments relative to four-year enrollments by 0.49 per-

Table 3.9. *Effect of Tuition on College Enrollment Composition: October CPS, 1979–88*

Panel A: All States

	Unweighted				Mean	Weighted				Mean
Two-year/four-year tuition[a]	−0.235	−0.247	−0.165	0.087	0.601	−0.282	−0.272	−0.067	0.122	0.552
	(0.040)	(0.041)	(0.046)	(0.079)		(0.029)	(0.031)	(0.041)	(0.057)	
Year dummies?	no	yes	yes	yes		no	yes	yes	yes	
Division dummies?	no	yes	yes	no		no	no	yes	no	
State dummies?	no	no	no	yes		no	no	no	yes	
R^2	0.211	0.221	0.294	0.696		0.416	0.431	0.526	0.840	

Note: There are 420 observations. See below for other regressors. The unweighted mean of the dependent variable is 0.28, weighted it is 0.34.

Panel B: By Region (Weighted)

	Northeast	Northcentral	South	West	Northeast	Northcentral	South	West
Two-year/four-year tuition[a]	0.251	−0.234	0.111	−0.596	−1.44	−0.459	−0.167	−0.934
	(0.081)	(0.110)	(0.089)	(0.081)	(0.639)	(0.724)	(0.506)	(0.216)
Relative tuition squared					1.20	0.157	0.268	0.413
					(0.451)	(0.501)	(0.480)	(0.245)
Year dummies	yes	yes	yes	yes	yes	yes	yes	yes
No. of observations	80	110	140	90	80	110	140	90
R^2	0.632	0.574	0.395	0.842	0.677	0.575	0.396	0.849

Note: Dependent variable = number of two-year/four-year enrollments (levels). Figures in parentheses represent standard errors. Other regressors include state-year percentages of: black; female; mother's education; father's education; family income; the ratio of average wages of those with some college to college graduates; the state unemployment rate; the average manufacturing wage; and the state income per capita. These variables are all weighted averages using the October CPS supplemental weights. The OLS estimates are weighted using the same weighted number of observations used to create the state-year averages. The weighted averages for relative tuition are: northeast = 0.62; northcentral = 0.69; south = 0.55; and west = 0.23.
[a] Relative tuition.

cent (evaluated at the means)—an effect that is larger than, but of a similar order of magnitude to, that estimated in Table 3.8 using the HSB. The effect increases slightly using the cross-section variation but falls significantly when I add census division dummies. Once I include both state and year dummies such that I estimate whether states that increased their two-year, relative to four-year, tuition more rapidly between 1979 and 1988 also experienced a greater shift toward two-year colleges, the coefficient on relative tuition becomes positive. Statistical significance of the effect depends on whether the regression is weighted.[28]

The basic experiment used to test the importance of tuition on college attendance is the variation in tuition rates across states. One implication of the difference between the within-division coefficients and the within-state coefficients is that such an experiment is not valid. Either the model varies by state or there are other omitted state factors that are correlated with both enrollment and tuition. On the other hand, there may just not be enough within-state variation in tuition to identify a price response with both time and state effects in the model. To examine these hypotheses more closely, I graphed relative tuition and relative enrollment in states where relative tuition changed by at least 30 percent in one year. The trends in the five states with such changes (Alabama, California, Maine, North Carolina, and Texas) are graphed in Figure 3.2. California had the most dramatic change, as community college tuition was raised from $0 to $30 in 1983. Within California, Maine, and North Carolina, the trends move roughly in opposite directions, supporting a price response, but they do not move so in Texas and Alabama. Again, the mixed results suggest caution when interpreting state variation as a natural experiment for tuition changes.

CONCLUSION

Evidence from the NLSY and the HSB suggests that students who attend junior colleges are more likely to be the first in their families to attend college and much less likely to have parents who graduated from four-year colleges than are students who first enroll in four-year schools. They are more likely to be nonblack, ceteris paribus, and they have much lower levels of measured ability. Junior colleges appear to provide a place in higher education for those not traditionally served by the four-year college system.

In addition, there is evidence that students considering junior colleges are "rational" decision makers who weigh the costs and benefits associ-

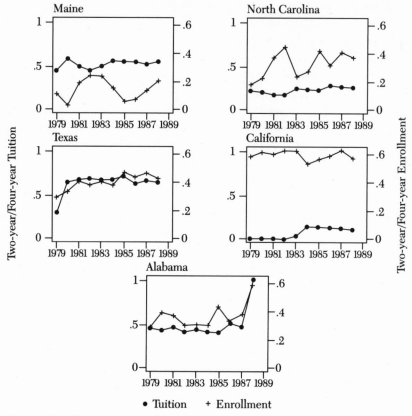

• Tuition   + Enrollment

Figure 3.2. *Relative Tuition and Enrollment, 1979–89*

ated with college attendance. They respond to changes in the returns to "some college" as well as to changes in two-year college tuition. In fact, most of the estimates presented suggest that changes in overall college tuition mainly affect two-year college enrollments. Simulations suggest that, at all levels of tuition, decreases in tuition primarily affect those who otherwise would not attend college. Two-year college proximity, however, appears equally to induce more people to attend college and to divert students from four-year colleges.

However, the NLSY and the HSB estimates primarily rely on state variation in tuition. Evidence from the CPS generally supports the importance of relative tuition for college enrollment composition, although it also suggests that state tuition levels may not be completely exogenous to enrollment decisions. Unfortunately, those interested in enrollment responses to college tuition have few other sources of natural variation. Important empirical issues that have not been adequately addressed, but would greatly contribute to higher education policy, are the sensitivity to two-year enrollments to changes in financial aid and the political economy of how states determine college tuition levels.

Table 3.1A. NLSY Sample Means and Standard Deviations

	No College		Two-Year College		Four-Year College	
Variables	Mean	S.D.	Mean	S.D.	Mean	S.D.
Female	0.4799	0.4998	0.5378	0.4989	0.5028	0.5003
Black	0.2242	0.4172	0.2119	0.4089	0.2105	0.4079
Test score	60.89	18.87	69.98	16.57	79.59	16.62
Family income[a]	21,283	14,445	26,671	16,649	31,268	18,768
Log of family size	0.3397	0.3298	0.2255	0.3442	0.1892	0.3593
Mother HS grad.	0.3872	0.4873	0.4963	0.5003	0.4551	0.4983
Mother some college	0.0638	0.2444	0.1333	0.3402	0.1570	0.3640
Mother college degree	0.0342	0.1818	0.0815	0.2738	0.1900	0.3925
Father HS grad.	0.3655	0.4817	0.3955	0.4893	0.3129	0.4639
Father some college	0.0789	0.2697	0.1363	0.3433	0.1524	0.3597
Father college grad.	0.0552	0.2285	0.1585	0.3655	0.3151	0.4648
Northeast	0.1940	0.3955	0.1630	0.3696	0.2036	0.4029
Northcentral	0.2821	0.4501	0.2222	0.4160	0.3151	0.4648
South	0.3419	0.4745	0.3422	0.4748	0.3527	0.4781
West	0.1821	0.3861	0.2726	0.4456	0.1286	0.3349
Central city	0.1775	0.3822	0.1704	0.3762	0.2184	0.4134
HS grads. avg. salary	7.70	0.57	7.77	0.63	7.67	0.52
Some college avg. salary	8.71	0.62	8.79	0.66	8.68	0.60
College grads. avg. salary	11.02	0.97	11.26	0.94	10.95	0.99
Estimated return to HS	0.2282	0.0466	0.2333	0.0487	0.2252	0.0440
Estimated return to some college	0.3473	0.0532	0.3551	0.0525	0.3445	0.0505
Estimated return to college	0.5460	0.0700	0.5534	0.0676	0.5459	0.0679
Two-year tuition	553	289	449	309	555	277
Four-year tuition	892	348	828	360	895	333
Unemployment rate	8.66	3.49	8.77	3.60	8.21	3.48
No. of two-year colleges per capita	0.0500	0.0196	0.0485	0.0195	0.0489	0.0184
No. of four-year colleges per capita	0.0704	0.0225	0.0644	0.0199	0.0712	0.0205
Educational expenditures per capita	675.58	90.11	686.52	89.46	676.78	87.01
State income per capita	11,406	1,416	11,820	1,363	11,342	1,409
% labor force in mfg.	0.2175	0.0549	0.2080	0.0527	0.2171	0.0562
No. of observations	1,521		675		879	

[a]In 1980 dollars.

APPENDIX 3.2

Table 3.2A. HSB Sample Means and Standard Deviations

Variables	No College		Two-Year College		Four-Year College	
	Mean	S.D.	Mean	S.D.	Mean	S.D.
Female	0.5461	0.4979	0.5697	0.4953	0.5611	0.4963
Black	0.2700	0.4440	0.1819	0.3859	0.2360	0.4247
Test score	44.80	7.75	48.47	8.04	54.12	8.11
Family income[a]	15,735	14,231	19,544	15,580	23,033	18,299
Family income missing	0.1467	0.3539	0.0909	0.2876	0.0878	0.2830
Mother's educ. missing	0.1601	0.3668	0.1207	0.3259	0.0695	0.2544
Mother HS grad.	0.3636	0.4811	0.3314	0.4708	0.3207	0.4668
Mother some college	0.0613	0.2399	0.1324	0.3391	0.1475	0.3547
Mother college grad.	0.0427	0.2022	0.0931	0.2906	0.1968	0.3977
Father's educ. missing	0.2548	0.4358	0.1941	0.3956	0.1560	0.3629
Father HS grad.	0.2149	0.4108	0.2101	0.4075	0.2036	0.4027
Father some college	0.0565	0.2309	0.1186	0.3234	0.1053	0.3070
Father college grad.	0.0565	0.2309	0.1425	0.3497	0.2613	0.4394
Northeast	0.1735	0.3788	0.1346	0.3413	0.2573	0.4372
Northcentral	0.2655	0.4418	0.1925	0.3944	0.2856	0.4518
South	0.4067	0.4913	0.3548	0.4786	0.3150	0.4646
West	0.1543	0.3613	0.3181	0.4659	0.1421	0.3492
Urban	0.2624	0.4400	0.2590	0.4382	0.2718	0.4449
HS grads. avg. salary	7.63	0.56	7.81	0.63	7.70	0.53
Some college avg. salary	8.64	0.58	8.84	0.64	8.72	0.57
College grads. avg. salary	10.85	1.01	11.29	0.99	11.05	1.01
Estimated return to HS	0.2071	0.0399	0.2130	0.0433	0.2073	0.0393
Estimated return to some college	0.3208	0.0450	0.3260	0.0444	0.3210	0.0460
Estimated return to college	0.5171	0.0608	0.5190	0.0565	0.5166	0.0624
Two-year tuition	510	260	393	292	544	279
Four-year tuition	826	315	718	353	865	318
Miles to two-year college	21.06	28.97	10.62	16.51	17.30	28.65
Miles to four-year college	21.18	25.24	18.02	23.34	15.03	20.76
Unemployment rate	7.70	2.75	7.43	2.62	7.53	2.65
State income per capita	10,712	1,285	11,320	1,211	11,019	1,226
No. of observations	2,904		1,880		2,962	

[a]In 1980 dollars.

Table 3.3A. October CPS Sample Means and Standard Deviations

	Unweighted		Weighted	
	Mean	*S.D.*	*Mean*	*S.D.*
Two-year/four-year enrollment	0.2793	0.1477	0.3387	0.1536
Two-year/four-year tuition	0.6016	0.1786	0.5518	0.2335
% Black	0.0794	0.0957	0.0943	0.0796
% Female	0.5300	0.1107	0.5285	0.0797
% Mother's educ. missing	0.0722	0.0591	0.0736	0.0464
% Mother HS grad.	0.4256	0.1217	0.4239	0.1094
% Mother some college	0.2212	0.1012	0.2137	0.0805
% Mother college grad.	0.2626	0.1100	0.2663	0.0805
% Father's educ. missing	0.1537	0.0844	0.1578	0.0681
% Father HS grad.	0.2774	0.1120	0.2613	0.0948
% Father some college	0.1698	0.0839	0.1654	0.0702
% Father college grad.	0.4530	0.1251	0.4707	0.0985
% Missing income	0.0567	0.0521	0.0565	0.0432
Avg. family income[a]	31,176	5,135	32,376	4,348
Some college/college grad. wage	0.7824	0.0494	0.7714	0.0411
Unemployment rate	7.225	2.347	7.329	2.207
Avg. manufacturing wage[b]	20.59	3.82	21.94	4.04
State income per capita[b]	11,441	1,812	12,298	1,798
New England	0.1190	0.3242	0.0604	0.2386
Middle Atlantic	0.0714	0.2578	0.1929	0.3950
East North Central	0.1190	0.3242	0.1967	0.3980
West North Central	0.1429	0.3503	0.0748	0.2635
South Atlantic	0.1429	0.3503	0.1452	0.3527
East South Central	0.0952	0.2939	0.0603	0.2383
West South Central	0.0952	0.2939	0.0938	0.2919
Mountain	0.1667	0.3731	0.0452	0.2081
Pacific	0.0476	0.2132	0.1306	0.3373
No. of observations	420		420 (26,359,814)[c]	

[a]Families of college students, in 1982 dollars.
[b]In 1982 dollars.
[c]Weighted.

Do Historically Black Institutions of Higher Education Confer Unique Advantages on Black Students? An Initial Analysis

Ronald G. Ehrenberg and Donna S. Rothstein

Throughout most of the late nineteenth and early twentieth centuries, the majority of black American citizens lived and were educated in the south. They were formally excluded from southern segregated white institutions of higher education and found higher educational opportunities only in Historically Black Institutions (HBIs).[1] Some HBIs (for example, Morehouse, Spelman, and Fisk) were private institutions that were initially established by church-related organizations. Others (for example, Florida A&M, Grambling, and Morgan State) were public institutions established in the southern states after the Civil War to provide separate education for black youths. In the absence of allowing blacks to attend the same institutions as whites, the establishment of the public HBIs was necessary if the southern states were to meet the requirements of the second (1890) Morrill Act. As part of providing funding for land grant institutions, the act required that the states provide educational opportunities for all of their citizens.

As the black population began to move to the north in response to urban industrial employment opportunities, the relative importance of the HBIs for the education of black college age students began to decline. The famous 1954 *Brown v. Board of Education* Supreme Court decision,

Ronald G. Ehrenberg is the Irving M. Ives Professor of Industrial and Labor Relations and Economics at Cornell University and a research associate at the National Bureau of Economic Research; Donna S. Rothstein is a Ph.D. candidate at Cornell University. We are grateful to Dan Goldhaber and Michael Schultheis for their research assistance, to David Card, William Spriggs, and William Brazziel for their comments, to the Andrew W. Mellon and William H. Donner Foundations for financial support, and to Alan Fechter and his staff at the National Research Council for providing us with the data used in section III of the paper. The views expressed here are solely our own and do not represent the views of Cornell University, the National Bureau of Economic Research, either foundation, the National Research Council, or any of the above-mentioned individuals.

which outlawed separate but equal public schools, actually had very little impact on many of the southern states, and formally segregated higher educational systems remained. When integrated at all, the white institutions often did so only as a result of legal suits pursued by the NAACP.[2] It was not until the passage of the 1964 Civil Rights Act, Title VI of which prohibited the allocation of federal funds to segregated public educational institutions, that any real progress at integration was made. However, this progress was very slow, and in the 1973 Supreme Court decision *Adams v. Richardson*, the southern states were formally and finally ordered to dismantle their dual higher educational systems.

As recently as 1964, over half of all bachelor's degrees granted to black Americans were granted by HBIs. By 1973, with the continued black migration to the north and the beginnings of integrated higher education in the south, the HBI share had fallen to about one-quarter to one-third, a range in which it remains today. The 105 institutions officially classified as HBIs that exist today are listed in Table 4.1. Over 90 percent of the institutions are four–year institutions, and over 95 percent of the students enrolled in HBIs attend four–year institutions. While more HBIs are private than public, the former are often quite small, and about three-quarters of the students at HBIs are enrolled in public institutions. Approximately 20 percent of all black college students are now enrolled in HBIs.

Despite the declining relative importance of HBIs in the production of black bachelor's degrees, in recent years they have become the subject of intense public policy debate for two reasons. First, court cases have been filed in a number of southern states that assert that black students continue to be underrepresented at traditionally white public institutions, that discriminatory admissions criteria are used by these institutions to exclude black students (e.g., basing admissions only on test scores and not also on grades), and that per student funding levels, program availability, and library facilities are substantially poorer at public HBIs than at other public institutions in these states (Johnson 1991). In one 1992 case, *United States v. Fordice*, the Supreme Court ruled that Mississippi had not done enough to eliminate racial segregation in its state-run higher educational institutions (Chira 1992). Rather than mandating a remedy, however, the Court sent the case back to the lower courts for action.

What should the appropriate action be? Should it be to integrate more fully both the historically white and the historically black institutions by breaking down discriminatory admissions practices at the former and establishing some unique programs at the latter? Should the HBIs be

Table 4.1. Historically Black Colleges and Universities, by Location and Year Founded

Alabama
Alabama A&M Univ. (Huntsville), 1875—U
Alabama State Univ. (Montgomery), 1874—U
Carver State Tech. College (Mobile), 1962—U2S
Concordia College (Selma), 1922—R2S
Fredd State Tech. College (Tuscaloosa), 1965—U2S
J. F. Drake State Tech. College (Huntsville), 1961—U2S
S. D. Bishop State Junior College (Mobile), 1927—U2
Lawson State College (Birmingham), 1965—U2
Miles College (Birmingham), 1905—RS
Oakwood College (Huntsville), 1896—R
Selma Univ. (Selma), 1876—RS
Stillman College (Tuscaloosa), 1876—RS
Talladega Univ. (Talladega), 1867—RS
Trenholm State Tech. College (Montgomery), 1966—U2S
Tuskegee Univ. (Tuskegee), 1881—R

Arkansas
Arkansas Baptist College (Little Rock), 1901—RS
Philander Smith College (Little Rock), 1877—RS
Shorter College (Little Rock), 1886—R2S
Univ. of Arkansas (Pine Bluff), 1873—U

Delaware
Delaware State College (Dover), 1891—U

District of Columbia
Howard Univ., 1867—R
Univ. of the District of Columbia, 1851—U

Florida
Bethune-Cookman College (Daytona Beach), 1904—R
Edward Waters College (Jacksonville), 1866—RS

Florida A&M Univ. (Tallahassee), 1877—U
Florida Memorial College (Miami), 1879—R

Georgia
Albany State College (Albany), 1903—U
Clark Atlanta Univ. (Atlanta), 1865—R
Fort Valley State College (Fort Valley), 1895—U
Interdenominational Theol. Center (Atlanta), 1958—R
Morehouse College (Atlanta), 1867—R
Morehouse School of Medicine (Atlanta), 1978—R
Morris Brown College (Atlanta), 1881—R
Paine College (Augusta), 1882—RS
Savannah State College (Savannah), 1890—U
Spelman College (Atlanta), 1881—R

Kentucky
Kentucky State Univ. (Frankfurt), 1886—U

Louisiana
Dillard Univ. (New Orleans), 1869—R
Grambling State Univ. (Grambling), 1901—U
Southern Univ. A&M College (Baton Rouge), 1880—U
Southern Univ. of New Orleans (New Orleans), 1959—U
Southern Univ. (Shreveport), 1964—U2
Xavier Univ. of Louisiana (New Orleans), 1915—R

Maryland
Bowie State College (Bowie), 1865—U
Coppin State College (Baltimore), 1900—U
Morgan State Univ. (Baltimore), 1867—U
Univ. of Maryland-Eastern Shore (Princess Anne), 1886—U

Michigan
Lewis College of Business (Detroit), 1874—R2S

Table 4.1. (continued)

Mississippi
Alcorn State Univ. (Lorman), 1871—U
Coahoma Junior College (Clarksdale),
    1949—U2
Jackson State Univ. (Jackson), 1877—U
Mary Holmes College (West Point),
    1892—R2S
Mississippi Valley State Univ. (Itta
    Bena), 1946—U
Rust College (Holly Springs), 1866—R
Tougaloo College (Tougaloo),
    1869—RS
Hinds Community College, Utica
    Campus, (Raymond), 1954—U2S

Missouri
Lincoln Univ. (Jefferson City),
    1866—U
Harris-Stowe State College (St.
    Louis), 1857—U

North Carolina
Barber-Scotia College (Concord),
    1867—RS
Bennett College (Greensboro),
    1873—RS
Elizabeth City State Univ. (Elizabeth
    City), 1891—U
Fayetteville State Univ. (Fayetteville),
    1877—U
Johnson C. Smith Univ. (Charlotte),
    1867—R
Livingstone College (Salisbury),
    1879—RS
North Carolina A&T State Univ.
    (Greensboro), 1891—U
North Carolina Central Univ.
    (Durham), 1910—U
Saint Augustine's College (Raleigh),
    1867—R
Shaw Univ. (Raleigh), 1865—R
Winston-Salem State Univ. (Winston-
    Salem), 1892—U

Ohio
Central State. Univ. (Wilberforce),
    1887—U
Wilberforce Univ. (Wilberforce),
    1856—RS

Oklahoma
Langston University (Langston),
    1897—U

Pennsylvania
Cheyney State Univ. (Cheyney),
    1838—U
Lincoln University (Lincoln), 1854—U

South Carolina
Allen Univ. (Columbia), 1870—RS
Benedict College (Columbia), 1870—R
Claflin College (Orangeburg),
    1869—RS
Clinton Junior College (Rock Hill),
    1894—R2S
Denmark Tech. College (Denmark),
    1948—U2S
Morris College (Sumter), 1908—RS
South Carolina State Univ.
    (Orangeburg), 1896—U
Voorhees College (Denmark),
    1897—RS

Tennessee
Fisk Univ. (Nashville), 1867—RS
Knoxville College (Knoxville),
    1875—R
Lane College (Jackson), 1882—RS
LeMoyne-Owen College (Memphis),
    1862—R
Meharry Medical College (Nashville),
    1876—R
Morristown College (Morristown),
    1881—R2
Tennessee State Univ. (Nashville),
    1912—U

Texas
Huston-Tillotson College (Dallas),
    1876—RS
Jarvis Christian (Hawkins), 1912—R
Paul Quinn College (Dallas), 1872—RS
Prairie View A&M Univ. (Prairie
    View), 1876—U
Saint Philip's College (San Antonio),
    1927—R2
Southwestern Christian College
    (Terrell), 1949—US
Texas College (Tyler), 1894—RS
Texas Southern Univ. (Houston),
    1947—U
Wiley College (Marshall), 1873—RS

U.S. Virgin Islands
College of the Virgin Islands (St.
    Thomas), 1962—U

Table 4.1. (continued)

Virginia	West Virginia
Hampton Univ. (Hampton), 1868—R	Bluefield State College (Bluefield),
Norfolk State Univ. (Norfolk), 1935—U	1895—U
Saint Paul's College (Lawrenceville),	West Virginia State College
1888—RS	(Institute), 1891—U
Virginia State Univ. (Petersburg),	
1882—U	
Virginia Union Univ. (Richmond),	
1865—R	

Source: 43 Code of Federal Regulations 608.2 (revised as of July 1, 1991), "What Institutions Are Eligible to Receive a Grant under the HBCU Program?" and Charleen M. Hoffman et al.
Note: U = public; R = private; 2 = two-year; 5 = 1990 fall enrollment < 1,000.

eliminated and their campuses either folded into the historically white institutions or abandoned? Or should effort be directed at equalizing per student expenditure levels and facilities between campuses, rather than at worrying about the racial distribution of students at each campus, even if such policies might result in "voluntary separate but equal" institutions?

From an economic efficiency perspective, the appropriate policy responses depend at least partially upon the answers to a number of questions: Do HBIs, per se, provide unique advantages to black students that they could not obtain at other institutions? If they do, is this because of the racial composition of their faculty or the racial composition of their students? If they do, would enrolling more black college students in higher expenditure per pupil integrated institutions actually leave these students in a worse position?

There is a long literature that stresses the importance of HBIs to black students, especially those from poorer socioeconomic and academic backgrounds. A summary of the literature is found in Pascarella and Terenzini (1991).[3] This literature suggests that students at HBIs are likely to have better self-images, be psychologically and socially better adjusted, and to have higher grades than their counterparts at other institutions. Although many studies have asserted that HBIs graduate a larger proportion of the black students that enroll in them than do other institutions, a much smaller number of studies have addressed (with mixed findings) whether HBIs continue to appear to enhance black students' degree probabilities once one controls for differences in the characteristics of the students that attend HBIs and other institutions. Only a handful have addressed whether attendance at an HBI, per se, enhances black students' subsequent labor market and educational success; these studies typically find that it does not. None of these studies takes account of the process by which black students decide to enroll (or are prevented from enrolling) in different types of institutions.

To shed some light on these issues, the next section presents econometric analyses of whether black college students who attended HBIs in the early 1970s had higher graduation rates, higher early career labor market success, and higher probabilities of attending graduate school than did their counterparts who attended other institutions. These analyses use data from the National Longitudinal Study of the High School Class of 1972 (NLS72). The econometric methods we employ control for characteristics of the students, characteristics of the institutions, and the above mentioned matching process between students and institutions.[4]

The second subject of policy debate relates to the production and employment of black doctorates (Ehrenberg 1992). Despite vigorous (or nonvigorous?) affirmative action efforts, the proportion of black faculty at major American universities is typically quite low. In part, this reflects the small number of black doctorates that are produced annually, and many people stress the need to increase the production of black doctorates to overcome this problem. Projections of forthcoming overall shortages of doctorates also reemphasize the need to increase black doctorate production to help avert these shortages, independent of concerns about the need for black faculty to serve as role models for black students.

What is the best way to increase the flow of black students into doctoral programs? Do HBIs currently serve disproportionately as the source of the black undergraduate students who go on for doctoral degrees? Should new doctoral programs be set up, or existing programs strengthened, at HBIs to enhance the flow of black doctorates? Or should attempts be made to recruit more black students from HBIs or from other institutions into existing doctoral programs at leading Research I institutions? In part, the appropriate policy responses depend on the answer to another question: Do those black undergraduate students from HBIs who go on to doctoral study and those who get doctoral degrees at HBIs fare as well in the academic labor market as do their counterparts from other institutions?

The third section provides partial answers to some of these questions by using special tabulations prepared for us from the National Research Council's Survey of Earned Doctorates. A brief concluding section summarizes the implications of our findings and suggests directions for future research.

DID HISTORICALLY BLACK INSTITUTIONS OF HIGHER
EDUCATION CONFER UNIQUE ADVANTAGES ON BLACK STUDENTS
IN THE 1970S?

This section presents a detailed description of our analyses of data on black college students from the NLS72. We focus on students who first enrolled in a four-year HBI or other four-year college within three years after their June 1972 graduation from high school.[5] Our interest is in learning whether attendance at an HBI per se increased the probability that these students received a bachelor's degree by 1979, improved their early (1979) labor market outcomes (as measured by earnings and an index of occupational prestige), and increased the probability that they subsequently enrolled in an advanced degree program.

These questions are all addressed in the context of models that permit the students' choice of college type (HBI or non-HBI) to be treated as endogenous. In places, the models also control for the process that determined whether an individual was employed in 1979. The sensitivity of our findings to the statistical models used are stressed throughout.

DESCRIPTIVE STATISTICS

Descriptive statistics for the 638 black students in our sample are found in Table 4.2. Forty-seven percent or 298, of these students attended HBIs at some time during the 1972–1979 period, while the remaining 340 students always attended other institutions.[6]

Mean SAT test scores (SAT) were substantially lower, and high school ranks (HSRANK) were somewhat poorer, for the students at HBIs. These students also tended to come from families with lower incomes (PARINC), and their parents were slightly less likely to have earned bachelor's degrees (DADBA, MOMBA). Not surprisingly, they were much more likely to have gone to high school in a state in the southeastern region of the country (SOUTH), where the majority of HBIs are located. Indeed, the proportion of full-time equivalent undergraduates enrolled in HBIs (SLOTS) in the states in which students went to high school was typically twice as large for students who subsequently enrolled in HBIs than it was for students who did not subsequently enroll in HBIs.

Characteristics of the high schools that the students attended also differed between the two groups. Students enrolled in HBIs were more likely to have attended a public high school (PUBHS), to have greater proportions of black high school classmates (BSTUDH) and black high

Ronald G. Ehrenberg and Donna S. Rothstein

Table 4.2. Descriptive Statistics: NLS72 Sample

	HBI Sample			Non-HBI Sample		
Variable	N	Mean	S.D.	N	Mean	S.D.
SAT	189	69.157	13.264	237	76.024	16.186
HSRANK	239	.402	.262	297	.372	.262
MALE	298	.399	.491	340	.368	.483
PAR INC	233	70.990	51.048	273	80.745	54.023
DADBA	294	.092	.289	335	.099	.298
MOMBA	295	.108	.312	338	.112	.316
DADSEI	243	30.432	18.359	289	29.904	18.273
BFACH	279	.400	.253	308	.235	.213
PUBHS	298	.919	.273	340	.882	.323
BSTUDH	279	.621	.318	308	.478	.325
COLL24	279	.445	.215	308	.448	.211
URBHS	279	.237	.426	308	.289	.454
SLOTS	298	.127	.077	340	.060	.078
SOUTH	298	.718	.451	340	.323	.469
CSAT	298	69.986	7.791	340	102.128	11.052
BFACC	255	.617	.131	317	.037	.043
BSTUDC	298	.925	.106	340	.100	.110
EXPST	298	27.362	12.005	340	31.295	21.209
PRIV	298	.332	.472	340	.274	.446
WAGE79	253	5.807	3.047	288	6.298	4.076
SEI79	253	43.415	17.067	288	45.829	17.641
BA79	298	.554	.498	340	.515	.501

*Sources:*Higher Education General Information Survey (HEGIS) (1972): EXPST, PRIV. SLOTS; HEGIS (1976): BSTUDC; Equal Employment Opportunity Commission (1989): BFACC; American Council on Education (1972): CSAT; NLS72: all other variables.
Where:

SAT   individual's total SAT score (divided by 10) (ACT scores converted to SAT scores using Astin's [1971] conversion method)
HSRANK   individual's high school rank (1 = lowest, 0 = highest)
MALE   1 = male, 0 = female
PARINC   parents' pretax income in 1972 (divided by 100)
DADBA   1 = father has a bachelor's degree, 0 = father does not have a bachelors' degree
MOMBA   1 = mother has a bachelor's degree, 0 = mother does not have a bachelor's degree
DADSEI   father's index of occupational prestige (10 = low, 90 = high)
PUBHS   1 = individual attended a public high school, 0 = other
BSTUDH   proportion of black students in the individual's high school
BFACH   proportion of black teachers in the individual's high school
COLL24   proportion of 1971 graduates at the individual's high school who went to two- or four-year colleges
URBHS   1 = urban high school, 0 = other
SLOTS   proportion of full-time equivalent undergraduate enrollment in HBIs in the individual's high school state
SOUTH   1 = went to high school in the southeast region, 0 = other
CSAT   average total SAT score of incoming freshmen at the individual's college (divided by 10)
BFACC   proportion of black faculty at the individual's college in 1989

Table 4.2. (continued)

BSTUDC	proportion of full-time equivalent black undergraduate students at the individuals's college
EXPST	educational and general expenditures per full-time equivalent student at the individual's college (divided by 100)
PRIV	1 = individual attended a private college, 0 = public college
WAGE79	individual's hourly earnings in 1979
SEI79	individual's index of occupational prestige in 1979
BA79	1 = individual received a bachelor's degree by 1979, 0 = did not receive a bachelor's degree by 1979

school teachers (BFACH), but were less likely to have gone to high school in an urban area (URBHS).

The characteristics of the colleges the students attended also differed. Mean SAT scores at the college or university in which the students enrolled (CSAT) were over 300 points lower in the HBI sample, while expenditures per full-time equivalent student (EXPST) averaged about 10 percent lower. The proportions of black students (BSTUDC) and black faculty (BFACC) at the students' institutions were both much higher in the HBI sample, and students at HBIs were more likely to be attending a private institution (PRIV).[7]

Turning to some of the outcomes that will be of interest to us, the proportion of students that had received a bachelor's degree by the 1979 survey data (BA79) was .04 higher in the HBI sample. In contrast, average hourly earnings for the roughly 85 percent of both samples that were employed in 1979 (WAGE79) was almost 10 percent lower in the HBI sample. An index of employed individuals' occupational prestige (SEI79) was also slightly lower for the HBI sample than for the non-HBI sample.[8]

One goal of our study was to estimate the effects of characteristics of colleges, other than whether they were HBIs, on students' educational and labor market outcomes. Of interest were questions such as: were outcomes higher at institutions that had greater expenditures per student and/or greater student test score selectivity? Were the advantages, if any, that can be attributed to HBIs due to the racial composition of the faculty or the racial composition of the students? Given that they historically have had different missions, did private HBIs benefit black students more or less than public HBIs did?

Our ability to answer such questions is limited by the high correlations that existed among these college characteristics; these correlations are tabulated in Table 4.3. It is clear that in the pooled sample we could not hope to disentangle the effects of HBIs from the effects of other variables. Similarly, in the non-HBI sample, the high correlations between CSAT

Table 4.3 College Characteristics Correlation Matrices

	CSAT	EXPST	BSTUDC	BFACC	PRIV
All (N = 638)					
HBI	.86	−.11	.97	.95	.06
CSAT		.40	−.86	−.83	.05
EXPST			−.16	−.11	.32
BSTUDC				.96	.08
BFACC					.06
HBI = 0 (N = 340)					
CSAT		.70	−.17	−.13	.34
EXPST			−.29	−.17	.30
BSTUDC				.56	−.00
BFACC					−.06
HBI = 1 (N = 298)					
CSAT		.33	−.29	−.18	−.00
EXPST			−.25	−.04	.43
BSTUDC				.44	.14
BFACC					−.01

Note: All variables are defined in Table 4.2.

and EXPST and between BSTUDC and BFACC made it unlikely that we could estimate the effects of the variables. Correlations are substantially lower in the HBI sample; and hence, throughout the paper, we attempt to estimate the effects of the various institutional characteristics on the different outcomes attained by students enrolled in HBIs.

THE DECISION TO ATTEND AN HBI

Prior attempts to estimate whether attendance at HBIs improves black students' graduation probabilities or labor market outcomes have, for the most part, treated whether a black student attended an HBI as exogenous (Thomas and Gordon 1985; Cross and Astin 1981; Pascarella et al. 1987; Pascarella, Smart, and Stoecker 1989). If students are not randomly assigned to HBIs, such a procedure may lead to biased coefficient estimates. As a first step, this section analyzes students' decisions to attend HBIs.

Given that a black student enrolled in a four-year institution, what determines whether it was an HBI? The answer is a complex one because it depends not only on the student's preferences and resources, but also on the policies pursued by institutions. For example, a number of southern states use scores on standardized tests as the sole criterion to gain admission to their historically white public institutions of higher education, in spite of the facts that black students often do poorly on these tests and that even the generators of the tests recommend that scores *not* be used as the only criterion for admissions decisions.

In the absence of being able to estimate a structural model in which we can identify both the admissions decision rules of all institutions and the preferences of each student, we adopt a simpler reduced form approach. A student's choice of institutional type, which resulted from his or her preferences and the constraints imposed by various institutions' decision rules, is assumed to have depended on the student's high school rank and SAT scores, characteristics of the student's family and of the high school that he or she attended, and the characteristics of the HBIs and the other higher educational institutions in the state in which the student attended high school.

Why consider the characteristics of only institutions in a single state? It is well known that, nationwide, the vast majority of students attend college in the same state in which they went to high school. As Table 4.4 indicates, this was true in the 1970s for students who attended HBIs as well. In 1976, 58 percent of the students enrolled in private HBIs, and 84 percent of the students enrolled in public HBIs, were in-state students.[9] Since roughly three-quarters of all students in HBIs attended public institutions, the overall in-state percentage was around 78.

Table 4.4 also contains a set of regression equations that seeks to explain the variation across HBIs in the proportion of freshmen that were in-state students. One key finding is that (holding the tuition level for out-of-state students constant) the lower was the tuition level for in-state students, the higher was the proportion of in-state students. In addition (other variables held constant, including tuition), private HBIs tended to attract a greater proportion of in-state students, and more selective HBIs tended to attract a smaller proportion of in-state students. These findings suggest several state-level institutional variables that should have influenced whether in-state students enrolled in an HBI in the state and, as described below, we include several in the model.

Table 4.5 presents probit estimates of our model of the determinants of whether an individual in our sample attended an HBI.[10] The only state-level variable included in the analyses reported in column 1 is SLOTS, the proportion of full-time equivalent undergraduate students in the student's high school state that were enrolled in HBIs.[11] The specification reported in column 2 adds three additional measures. RELTUI is the average (weighted by full-time equivalent [FTE] enrollments) tuition in HBIs in the state relative to the weighted average tuition for other institutions in the state. RELFAC is the weighted average proportion of

Table 4.4. *Determinants of the Proportion of Freshmen at HBIs That Are In-State Students*
(Absolute Value of t Statistic)

	(1)		(2)		(3)		(4)	
	Fall '76	Fall '88	Fall '76	Fall '88	Fall '76	Fall '88	Fall '76	Fall '88
INT	.963 (16.3)	.803 (9.5)	.740 (3.7)	.447 (2.3)	.939 (13.5)	.760 (6.3)	.839 (3.7)	.591 (2.4)
PRIV	.095 (1.0)	.219 (1.9)	.064 (0.7)	.222 (2.0)	.169 (1.5)	.240 (1.7)	.153 (1.4)	.247 (1.7)
TUIN[a]	-.361 (3.5)	-.238 (3.3)	-.314 (2.8)	-.236 (3.3)	-.481 (4.0)	-.255 (2.8)	-.461 (3.6)	-.256 (2.8)
TUOUT[a]			.031 (0.4)	.075 (1.2)			.085 (1.0)	.113 (1.4)
RAT84	.031 (0.4)	.069 (1.1)	.235 (1.2)	.071 (2.1)	.096 (1.2)	.113 (1.4)	.022 (0.6)	.034 (0.8)
19 State dummies included?	no	no	no	no	yes	yes	yes	yes
N	89	94	89	94	89	94	89	94
R²	.395	.412	.391	.426	.526	.468	.515	.458

Sources: *Barron's Profile of American Colleges* (Woodbury, NY: Barron's Educational Service, 1984): RAT84; National Center for Education Statistics (NCES), Higher Education General Information System (HEGIS) (1976), and Integrated Postsecondary Educational Data System (IPEDS) (1988): Residence and Migration of College Students (1988); PSAME; HEGIS (1976) and IPEDS: Institutional Characteristics (1988): PRIV, TUIN, TUOUT.

Note: Also included are dummy variables for nonreporting of tuition levels and, in columns 2 and 4, absence of a selectivity rating. The weighted mean proportions of students that were in-state students (PSAME) in 1976 and 1988, respectively, were .58 and .37 in the private HBIs, and .84 and .74 in the public HBIs.

Where:

INT   intercept
PRIV   1 = private institution, 0 = public
TUIN   tuition level if private, in-state tuition level if public
TUOUT   tuition level if private, out-of-state tuition level if public
RAT84   Barron's 1984 selectivity rating of the institution (4 = competitive, 5 = less competitive, 6 = noncompetitive)
PSAME   proportion of freshmen that are in-state students

[a]Coefficients have been multiplied by 1,000.

Table 4.5. *Probit Estimates of the Decision to Attend an HBI (Absolute Value of* t *Statistic)*

	(1)	(2)
SLOT	5.780 (7.2)	3.841 (3.8)
HSRANK	.310 (1.2)	.292 (1.1)
PUBHS	.434 (2.3)	.354 (1.8)
BFACH	1.020 (2.3)	1.016 (2.2)
BSTUDH	.216 (0.7)	.217 (0.7)
COLL24	.279 (0.9)	.612 (1.9)
URBHS	.129 (0.9)	.200 (1.2)
SAT	$-.017$ (3.4)	$-.018$ (3.4)
MALE	.202 (1.7)	.201 (1.7)
MOMBA	.014 (0.1)	$-.077$ (0.4)
DADBA	$-.049$ (0.2)	.111 (0.5)
DADSEI	.005 (1.2)	.001 (1.4)
PARINC	$-.001$ (0.4)	.000 (0.1)
RELTUI		.497 (1.9)
RELFAC		.009 (1.2)
RELSAT		$-.738$ (0.6)
χ^2/DOF	170.142/20	197.386/25
N	638	638

Note: Also included in the equation are dichotomous variables for nonreporting of high school rank; SAT scores; other high school characteristics; mother's and father's education; father's occupational status; parents' family income in 1972; and, in column 2, the absence of HBIs in the student's state of residence in 1972 and the absence of data on black faculty in a state that has at least one HBI.

Where:

SAT	individual's total SAT score (ACT scores converted to SAT scale) if reported, 0 = SAT not reported
RELTUI	average (weighted by FTE enrollments) tuition in HBIs in the student's high school state relative to average (weighted) tuition in other institutions in the state
RELFAC	average (weighted) proportion of black faculty in HBIs in the state relative to the average (weighted) proportion of black faculty in other institutions in the state
RELSAT	average (weighted) SAT score of HBIs in the state relative to the average (weighted) SAT score of other institutions in the state

All other variables are defined in Table 4.2.

black faculty in HBIs in the state relative to the weighted average proportion of black faculty in other institutions in the state. Finally, RELSAT is the weighted average SAT score in HBIs in the state relative to the weighted average SAT scores of other institutions in the state. Our expectation is that these variables, respectively, should be negatively, positively, and positively related to the probability of enrollment in an HBI.

The estimates in Table 4.5 suggest that students with higher test scores were less likely to attend HBIs. Students from public high schools and high schools with a greater proportion of black teachers were more likely to attend HBIs. Males were more likely to attend HBIs than were females. Finally, parents' educational backgrounds and income do not appear to have influenced the students' decision to attend an HBI.

The fraction of full-time equivalent undergraduate student slots in a state that were available in HBIs also mattered. While the other state-level variables proved to be jointly significant when included in the model, individually only RELTUI approached statistical significance, and its coefficient was positive. Higher levels of RELTUI may have signified increased relative quality of HBIs in a way not captured by SAT scores and, thus, may have led to an increased probability of black students' enrollment in an HBI.

THE CHARACTERISTICS OF THE COLLEGES STUDENTS ATTENDED

Characteristics of colleges, other than whether they are HBIs, may influence a student's educational and early labor market outcomes. The quality of an institution (as measured by its expenditure per student) or the quality of its students (as measured by their average test scores) have been shown to matter (James et al. 1989). Within the HBI sector, the proportions of students and faculty that were black varied considerably, and if HBIs did prove to confer unique advantages on black students, it is important to learn whether it was the racial mix of the students and/or that of the faculty that was responsible.[12] Finally, as noted at the start of this chapter, private and public HBIs may have had differential impacts on students. Thus, in some specifications, we include each of these variables in the educational and labor market outcome equations that appear in subsequent sections.

Of course, the characteristics of institutions chosen by students are not random, and it is of some interest to understand how individuals are matched to institutional characteristics. Table 4.6 provides such estimates for individuals enrolled in HBIs and those individuals enrolled in other institutions. The characteristics analyzed are the average SAT score in the institution (CSAT), institutional expenditures per student (EXPST), the proportions of black faculty (BFACC) and students (BSTUDC), and whether the institution was private (PRIV).[13] In each case, the characteristic was assumed to depend on the weighted mean value across institutions in the sector in the state in which the individual went to high school of the same characteristic, as well as a vector of characteristics of the individual, his or her family, and the high school that he or she attended.

Not surprisingly, given that most individuals remained in the same state for college, the mean values of the state/sector characteristics prove to be important predictors. In addition, more able students, as measured by higher test scores and class rank, enrolled in institutions with higher average test scores and higher expenditures per student. For students not enrolled in HBIs, an increase in their test scores also was associated with lower proportions of black students and black faculty in the institution that the students attended. For students enrolled in HBIs, an increase in the proportion of black teachers in their high school was associated with an increase in the proportion of black faculty in their college. Finally, if a student graduated from high school in a state that had no HBIs and he or she attended an HBI, other variables held constant, the student tended to be enrolled in an HBI with higher average test scores, expenditures per student, proportions of black faculty and black students, and probability of being private. These latter findings suggest some of the institutional characteristics that black families who sent their children out of state to HBIs were interested in obtaining.

RECEIPT OF A BACHELOR'S DEGREE BY 1979

The proportions of students who received bachelor's degrees by 1979 were .554 in the HBI sample and .515 in the non-HBI sample (see Table 4.2). What happens to the difference in these proportions once one controls for differences between the two groups in the characteristics of individuals and of the schools they attended, as well as the process by which students enrolled in HBIs or other schools?

Table 4.7 presents probit estimates of the probability that a bachelor's degree was received by 1979. Equations were estimated for students who attended HBIs, students who attended other institutions, and the pooled sample. In the separate sample cases, specifications were reported in which the probability was assumed to have varied with measures of the individual's ability and family background, and then the probability was assumed to have varied with these variables plus the characteristics of the college the individual attended. The pooled analyses included a dichotomous variable for whether the individual attended an HBI and also specifications in which this variable was treated as endogenous. To accomplish the latter, instruments for the student's institutional type were obtained from the choice of sector equations reported in Table 4.5 (see Maddala 1983).

Turning first to the estimates by sector, students whose high school class rank was better were more likely to have received a degree in both

Table 4.6. Determinants of the Characteristics of the Colleges Attended
(Absolute Value of t Statistic)

	CSAT		EXPST		BFACC		BSTUDC		PRIV[a]	
	OTHER	HBI	OTHER	HBI	OTHER	HBI	OTHER	HBI	OTHER	HBI
MALE	1.708 (1.6)	.684 (0.8)	2.162 (0.9)	−.041 (0.0)	.001 (0.2)	.002 (0.2)	−.021 (1.7)	−.008 (1.7)	.100 (0.5)	−.106 (1.1)
HSRANK	−4.886 (2.1)	−3.853 (2.0)	−5.629 (1.1)	−4.937 (1.6)	−.007 (0.6)	.023 (0.6)	−.019 (0.7)	.029 (1.1)	−.853 (2.2)	.565 (1.3)
SAT	.199 (4.5)	.048 (1.2)	.351 (3.8)	.190 (3.0)	−.000 (1.6)	−.000 (0.6)	−.963 (1.9)[b]	.761 (1.4)[b]	.005 (0.7)	.005 (0.6)
PARINC	−.004 (0.4)	−.004 (0.4)	−.024 (1.0)	.029 (1.8)	.000 (0.4)	−.000 (0.1)	−.000 (0.5)	.061 (0.5)	−.002 (1.3)	.003 (1.2)
DADSEI	−.014 (0.4)	.043 (1.6)	−.080 (1.0)	−.002 (0.0)	.038 (2.0)[b]	.096 (0.2)[b]	−.001 (1.2)	−.000 (0.5)	.013 (2.2)	−.009 (1.4)
MOMBA	4.259 (2.3)	−2.210 (1.4)	7.748 (2.0)	−2.972 (1.2)	.014 (1.5)	.002 (0.6)	.023 (1.1)	.022 (1.1)	.064 (0.2)	−.528 (1.6)
DADBA	1.058 (0.5)	1.173 (0.6)	−1.384 (0.3)	3.634 (1.2)	−.002 (0.2)	−.026 (0.8)	−.002 (0.9)	−.010 (0.5)	−.237 (0.3)	.333 (0.8)
PUBHS	−1.141 (0.7)	−3.066 (2.0)	−1.967 (0.6)	−4.417 (1.8)	.009 (1.6)	.010 (0.3)	.038 (2.0)	.020 (1.0)	−.290 (1.2)	−.416 (1.3)
BFACH	5.966 (1.4)	−1.266 (0.5)	13.877 (1.6)	−5.500 (1.2)	.019 (0.9)	.002 (0.0)	.005 (0.1)	.087 (2.2)	.172 (0.3)	.732 (1.2)
BSTUDH	−1.693 (0.6)	.230 (0.1)	−1.850 (0.3)	3.003 (0.8)	−.019 (1.4)	−.024 (0.5)	−.019 (0.6)	−.044 (1.4)	.391 (0.9)	−.693 (1.4)
COLL24	6.057 (2.1)	1.638 (0.8)	7.076 (1.1)	−.350 (0.1)	.027 (1.9)	−.076 (1.9)	.002 (0.1)	−.054 (1.9)	.917 (1.9)	−.142 (0.3)
URBHS	−.481 (0.3)	.969 (0.8)	−2.574 (1.0)	−2.038 (0.7)	.008 (1.3)	.021 (1.0)	.049 (3.3)	−.003 (0.2)	−.267 (1.3)	.603 (2.4)
OSAT	1.027 (7.1)									
OEXP			1.208 (5.9)							
OPBF					.763 (3.0)					
OPBS							1.130 (5.4)			
OPRIV									1.801 (3.4)	

	(1)	(2)	(3)	(4)	(5)	(6)
HSAT	.617 (9.3)	.496 (8.3)	.868 (8.0)	.614 (9.0)	2.780 (5.7)	1.266 (3.5)
HEXP						
HPBF						
HPBS						
HPRIV	45.299 (9.1)	16.476 (4.9)	.541 (7.3)	.520 (8.1)		
HDV						
$\bar{R}^2$/DOF	.319/319	.190/319	.298/276	.029/296	.104/319	.274/276
χ^2/DOF	.213/276	.207/232			48.019/20	64.121/21

Note: Also included in each equation are dichotomous variables for nonreporting of high school rank; SAT; parents' income; father's occupational prestige; mother's and father's educational level; high school characteristics; and, in BFACC equation for HBIs, black faculty.

Where:

HSAT   average (weighted) SAT score in HBIs in the student's high school state (divided by 10), 0 if no HBIs in the state

HEXP   average (weighted) expenditure per pupil in the student's high school state (divided by 100), 0 if no HBIs in the state

HPBF   average (weighted) proportion of black faculty in HBIs in the state, 0 if no HBIs in the state

HPBS   average (weighted) proportion of black students in HBIs in the state, 0 if no HBIs in the state

HPRIV   average (weighted) proportion of students in the student's high school state in HBIs who are in private institutions, 0 if no HBIs in the state

HDV   1 = no HBI's in the student's high school state, 0 = otherwise

OSAT, OEXP, OPBF, OPBS, OPRIV are similarly defined save that they refer to institutions other than HBIs.

All other variables are defined in Table 4.2.

a Probit analyses.

b Coefficient has been multiplied by 1,000.

Table 4.7. Probit Estimates of Probability That Bachelor's Degree Received by 1979 (Absolute Value of t Statistic)

	Students at HBIs		Other Students		Pooled–All Students	Pooled–All Students HBI Endogenous	
	(1H)	(2H)	(1O)	(2O)	(1A)	(1/1)[a]	(1/2)[b]
MALE	−.051 (0.3)	−.013 (0.1)	−.217 (1.4)	−.238 (1.5)	−.132 (1.2)	−.151 (1.4)	−.149 (1.4)
SAT	.008 (1.0)	.010 (1.2)	.020 (3.1)	.016 (2.3)	.015 (3.1)	.018 (3.5)	.018 (3.5)
HSRANK	−1.239 (3.4)	−1.275 (3.5)	−.950 (2.9)	−1.011 (2.1)	−1.085 (4.6)	−1.077 (4.5)	−1.079 (4.5)
MOMBA	.533 (1.7)	.493 (1.6)	.354 (1.3)	.406 (1.4)	.449 (2.3)	.437 (2.2)	.435 (2.2)
DADBA	−.236 (0.7)	−.238 (0.7)	−.118 (0.4)	−.149 (0.5)	−.159 (0.7)	−.173 (0.7)	−.177 (0.8)
DADSEI	−.002 (0.4)	−.002 (0.3)	.014 (2.5)	.014 (2.4)	.217 (1.2)	.006 (1.4)	.005 (1.4)
PARINC[a]	.328 (1.8)	.367 (1.8)	−.095 (0.6)	−.060 (0.7)	.088 (0.7)	.105 (0.8)	.102 (0.8)
HBI					.254 (2.3)	.615 (2.5)	.604 (2.7)
CSAT		−.015 (1.3)		.002 (0.2)			
PRIV		.174 (0.9)		.144 (0.8)			
BFACC		−1.049 (1.5)		−1.657 (0.6)			
BSTUDC		−.179 (0.2)		−1.069 (1.1)			
EXPST		−.006 (0.7)		.003 (0.6)			
χ²/DOF	35.002 (13)	40.573 (19)	57.544 (13)	66.908 (19)	83.641 (14)	84.457 (14)	85.438 (14)

Note: Also included in each equation are dichotomous variables for nonreporting of SAT; high school rank; mother's and father's education levels; father's occupational prestige index; parents' income; and, in (2), proportion of black faculty in 1990 at the institution.
Where:
HBI 1 = student attended a historically black institution, 0 = student attended another institution
All other variables are defined in Table 4.2.
[a]Instrument for HBI derived from Table 4.5, column 1.
[b]Instrument for HBI derived from Table 4.5, column 2.

sectors. Higher SAT scores were associated with higher completion probabilities as well, but the relationship is statistically significant only for students who did not attend HBIs. Students from wealthier families, as measured by higher family income or higher father's occupational prestige, had higher completion probabilities, as did students from families where the mother had a bachelor's degree.

When one adds institutional characteristics to the analysis, they prove not to be statistically significant as a group in each sector; individually, no single characteristic was statistically significant either.[14] One cannot infer from these results, therefore, that increasing institutional selectivity, expenditure per student, or the proportions of black students or faculty increased black students' completion probabilities in either sector. Nor were private institutions associated with higher completion rates than those of public institutions. Turning to the pooled analyses, the results in column 1A clearly indicate that, holding other factors constant, the probability that a bachelor's degree was received by 1979 was significantly higher if the student attended an HBI than if the student attended another institution. Indeed, one can make use of the coefficient estimates from column 1A and the values of the explanatory variables for each individual to compute how much higher the probability would have been for each individual if he or she had attended an HBI.[15] When this is done, the mean value of these differentials is .090, and the standard deviation of the differentials is only .015. This is strong evidence that the probability of these black students receiving a bachelor's degree by 1979 was higher if they attended HBIs than if they attended other institutions.[16]

The estimates in column 1A do not control for the fact that enrollment in an HBI was not a random occurrence. To do so, we compute instrumental variable estimates for the probability that a student was enrolled in an HBI from each of the two enrollment models found in Table 4.5. We then reestimate the graduation probability model twice, replacing the dichotomous HBI variable in turn by each of the instruments. The resulting estimates appear in columns 1I1 and 1I2 of Table 4.7.

The latter two sets of coefficients prove to be virtually identical. The coefficients of the HBI instrument in both cases are much larger than the original HBI coefficient found in column 1A. Indeed, when one computes the implied impacts of attending an HBI in these models, as described above, one finds that the mean probabilities of obtaining a bachelor's degree by 1979 were over .20 higher in each of these two models if the individual attended an HBI. That is, controlling for the endogeneity of whether these students attended an HBI substantially increased our estimate of the HBI/non-HBI probability of graduating by 1979 differential.

Given that we obtained virtually identical estimates when the two different instruments for attendance at HBIs were used, for simplicity, in the remainder of the chapter, we report results only for the instrument derived from the specification that excludes the relative characteristics from the enrollment equation (Table 4.5, column 1).

EARLY CAREER EARNINGS

Table 4.8 presents estimates of the logarithm of 1979 hourly earnings equations for individuals who initially were enrolled in HBIs, but who were employed in 1979 and not enrolled full-time in college. Missing from this sample then is full-time undergraduate or graduate students and/or individuals who were unemployed or not in the labor force. Table 4.9 presents similar estimates for individuals who were initially enrolled in other institutions.

Equations were estimated that both excluded and included whether the individual had received a bachelor's degree by 1979. For each of these cases, since enrollment in an HBI was nonrandom, specifications were also estimated that controlled for the factors that determined whether an individual enrolled in an HBI, using the sample selection bias correction method suggested by Heckman (1979).[17] As is well known, this involves computing, and then adding, an estimated correction factor (the inverse Mills' ratio) to the model and then reestimating the models.

Since employment in 1979 was also a nonrandom event, specifications were also estimated that controlled for the probability that each individual was observed employed. These latter specifications made use of estimated employment status equations and were estimated under the assumption that the correction factors for attendance at an HBI and employment in 1979 were independent of each other.[18]

The explanatory variables included in these models were personal and family characteristics of the individual, the area unemployment rate in 1979, and, to control for price differences across areas, a vector of regional dichotomous variables and a dichotomous variable that indicates whether the individual attended an urban high school. The high school urbanization variable served as a proxy for the extent of urbanization in the area in which the individual resided in 1979. Some specifications also included the characteristics of the college that the student attended. However, in neither sector did any of these college characteristics appear to significantly influence early career wages.

Table 4.8. Logarithm of 1979 Hourly Earnings Equations: HBI Students (Absolute Value of t Statistic)

	OLS				Selectivity Corrected			
	(1)	(2)	(3)	(4)	(1A)	(2A)	(3A)	(4A)
MALE	.283 (4.7)	.271 (4.3)	.277 (4.8)	.259 (4.4)	.282 (4.6)	.304 (4.9)	.279 (4.8)	.298 (5.0)
SAT	.002 (0.1)	.002 (0.6)	.001 (0.4)	.001 (.03)	.002 (.06)	.002 (0.6)	.001 (0.2)	.001 (0.2)
HSRANK	-.350 (2.6)	-.328 (2.4)	-.252 (2.0)	-.220 (1.7)	-.349 (2.7)	-.336 (2.5)	-.252 (2.0)	-.249 (2.0)
URBHS	.107 (1.5)	.111 (1.4)	.131 (1.9)	.138 (1.9)	.108 (1.5)	.121 (1.6)	.131 (1.9)	.141 (2.0)
MOMBA	-.177 (1.7)	-.167 (1.6)	-.228 (2.3)	-.215 (2.1)	-.178 (1.7)	-.230 (2.1)	-.227 (2.3)	-.267 (2.6)
DADBA	.141 (1.2)	.135 (1.1)	.176 (1.5)	.167 (1.2)	.143 (1.2)	.110 (0.9)	.174 (1.5)	.147 (1.3)
DADSEI[a]	-.476 (0.2)	-.387 (0.2)	-.319 (0.2)	-.396 (0.2)	-.001 (0.2)	-.000 (0.2)	-.000 (0.1)	-.000 (0.1)
PARINC[a]	.794 (1.0)	.662 (0.9)	.519 (0.8)	.349 (0.5)	.001 (1.0)	.001 (1.4)	.000 (0.7)	.001 (1.0)
UNEMP	7.866 (2.0)	7.569 (1.9)	5.409 (1.4)	4.983 (1.3)	7.818 (2.0)	10.248 (2.5)	5.478 (1.4)	7.499 (1.9)
CSAT		.001 (0.1)		.002 (0.5)				
PRIV		.020 (0.3)		-.016 (0.2)				
BFACC		.313 (1.1)		.353 (1.3)				
BSTUDC		-.345 (1.1)		-.352 (1.2)				
EXPST		.001 (0.2)		.002 (0.6)				
BA79			.298 (5.3)	.310 (5.5)			.300 (5.3)	.282 (5.0)
λ (HBI)					-.014 (0.2)	-.006 (0.1)	.024 (0.2)	.031 (0.4)
λ (EMP)						-.395 (1.9)		.320 (1.6)
R̄²	.121	.109	.216	.211	.118	.128	.212	.218
N	253	253	253	253	253	253	253	253

Note: Each equation also includes seven regional dichotomous variables (to control for cost of living) and dichotomous variables for the nonreporting of SAT, high school rank, high school characteristics, mother's and father's education levels, father's occupational status, and parental income.

Where:

UNEMP 1979 unemployment rate in the individual's state of residence

BA79 1 = received a bachelor's degree by 1979, 0 = did not receive a degree by 1979

λ (HBI) inverse Mills' ratio for attendance at HBI

λ (EMP) inverse Mills' ratio for employed in 1979

[a]Coefficient has been multiplied by 1,000.

Table 4.9. *Logarithm of 1979 Hourly Earnings Equations: Non-HBI Students*
(Absolute Value of t Statistic)

	OLS				Selectivity Corrected			
	(1)	(2)	(3)	(4)	(1A)	(2A)	(3A)	(4A)
MALE	.157 (2.9)	.155 (2.8)	.173 (3.2)	.172 (3.1)	.174 (3.2)	.194 (3.5)	.190 (3.5)	.207 (3.7)
SAT	.001 (0.4)	.001 (0.3)	.000 (0.1)	.000 (0.1)	-.001 (0.3)	-.000 (0.1)	-.002 (0.7)	-.001 (0.4)
HSRANK	-.150 (1.3)	-.132 (1.0)	-.097 (0.8)	-.076 (0.6)	-.146 (1.3)	-.118 (1.0)	-.092 (0.8)	-.073 (0.6)
URBHS	.229 (3.7)	.230 (3.6)	.229 (3.7)	.228 (3.6)	.228 (3.7)	.236 (3.8)	.228 (3.7)	.235 (3.8)
MOMBA	-.076 (0.8)	-.090 (0.9)	-.097 (1.0)	-.113 (1.2)	-.087 (0.9)	-.103 (1.1)	-.108 (1.2)	-.120 (1.4)
DADBA	.119 (1.1)	.120 (1.0)	.127 (1.1)	.128 (1.2)	.159 (1.5)	.113 (1.0)	.168 (1.6)	.124 (1.1)
DADSEI[a]	.001 (0.7)	.002 (0.7)	.001 (0.4)	.001 (0.5)	.002 (1.1)	.002 (1.2)	.002 (0.8)	.002 (1.0)
PARINC[a]	.002 (2.7)	.002 (2.6)	.002 (2.8)	.002 (2.8)	.001 (2.4)	.001 (2.5)	.001 (2.6)	.002 (2.7)
UNEMP	1.036 (0.2)	1.584 (0.3)	1.690 (0.4)	2.284 (0.5)	2.506 (0.6)	4.367 (1.0)	3.176 (0.8)	4.783 (1.1)
CSAT		-.001 (0.2)		-.001 (0.3)				
PRIV		.012 (0.2)		.004 (0.1)				
BFACC		1.035 (1.0)		1.130 (1.1)				
BSTUDC		-.187 (0.5)		-.145 (2.7)				
EXPST		.002 (0.9)		.002 (0.8)				
BA79			.141 (2.7)	.143 (2.7)			.142 (2.7)	.126 (2.4)
λ (HBI)					.238 (2.4)	.241 (2.4)	.240 (2.4)	.241 (2.4)
λ (EMP)						-.291 (1.7)		-.261 (1.6)
R̄²	.104	.089	.124	.111	.119	.127	.140	.145
N	288	288	288	288	288	288	288	288

Note: See footnote to Table 4.8 for the other variables included in the model.
[a]Coefficient has been multiplied by 1,000.

Our interest in these equations is primarily for the purpose of computing estimates from them as to whether individuals who attended HBIs earned more than they would have earned if they had attended other institutions. We make such estimates in a later subsection. For now, we note only two findings. First, the return to earning a bachelor's degree by 1979 was higher for individuals who attended HBIs than for other individuals. Second, correction for both types of sample selection bias appear important for individuals who did not attend HBIs, and correction for selection bias associated with employment status appears important for individuals who attended HBIs.

Table 4.10 presents estimates of wage equations when the data for individuals who attended both HBIs and other institutions were pooled together, and a dichotomous variable for attendance at an HBI was added to the model. The $-.021$ coefficient of this variable in column 1, which is statistically insignificantly different from zero, suggests that enrollment in an HBI did *not* lead to an increase in early career earnings for black college students in the sample. This conclusion continues to hold when the sample selection bias correction method is used to control for being employed (column 1A), when enrollment at an HBI is treated as endogenous and an instrumental variable estimate used instead of the actual value (column 1B), and when the instrumental variable and the sample selection bias correction method are used simultaneously (column 1C). That is, we find no evidence that attendance at an HBI led, on average, to increased 1979 hourly earnings.[19]

What if we add whether an individual received a bachelor's degree by 1979 to the model, treat the degree attainment and wage equations as recursive, and estimate the augmented wage equation? The coefficient of HBI becomes $-.036$ and remains statistically insignificant. However, attainment of a bachelor's degree raises the logarithm of earnings by a statistically significant .214. Since individuals who attended HBIs were more likely to graduate, one may ask whether this positive indirect effect of HBIs on earnings was larger than the negative direct effect of attendance at an HBI.

The answer is no. The analogous (single-equation) estimate of the marginal impact of attending an HBI on degree attainment by 1979 was .090, and thus the total effect of attendance at an HBI on 1979 earnings is estimated in percentage terms as $-.017$ ($[.214][.090]-.036$). Similar findings occur (column 3C) when we control for both the endogeneity of HBI and for sample selection (employment) bias. With attendance at HBI treated as endogenous, the estimated mean impact of attendance at an HBI on degree attainment was .215. Hence, the estimated total effect

Table 4.10. Logarithm of 1979 Hourly Earnings Equations: All Students (Absolute Value of t Statistic)

	OLS			Selectivity Corrected					
	(1)	(2)	(3)	(1A)	(1B)	(1C)	(3A)	(3B)	(3C)
MALE	.204 (5.2)	.218 (5.7)	.213 (5.6)	.222 (5.6)	.208 (5.3)	.225 (3.6)	.232 (6.0)	.224 (5.8)	.237 (6.1)
SAT	.001 (0.9)	.001 (0.3)	.001 (0.4)	.002 (1.1)	.001 (0.4)	.001 (0.8)	.001 (0.5)	-.000 (0.3)	.000 (0.1)
HSRANK	-.264 (3.1)	-.185 (2.2)	-.190 (2.2)	-.242 (2.8)	-.265 (3.1)	-.242 (2.8)	-.173 (2.0)	-.185 (2.2)	-.173 (2.0)
URBHS	.182 (4.0)	.188 (4.2)	.193 (4.3)	.194 (4.2)	.182 (4.0)	.194 (4.2)	.197 (4.3)	.187 (4.2)	.197 (4.3)
MOMBA	-.129 (1.9)	-.161 (2.5)	-.161 (2.5)	-.153 (2.3)	-.130 (1.9)	-.155 (2.3)	-.177 (2.7)	-.162 (2.4)	-.180 (2.7)
DADBA	.126 (1.6)	.140 (1.8)	.145 (1.9)	.085 (1.0)	.130 (1.7)	.088 (1.1)	.107 (1.4)	.146 (1.9)	.110 (1.4)
DADSEI	.001 (0.5)	.000 (0.1)	.000 (0.3)	.001 (0.6)	.001 (0.6)	.001 (0.8)	.000 (0.2)	.000 (0.3)	-.001 (0.5)
PARINC	.001 (2.7)	.001 (2.7)	.001 (2.5)	.001 (2.9)	.001 (2.5)	.001 (2.8)	.001 (2.8)	.001 (2.5)	.001 (2.7)
UNEMP	3.961 (1.4)	3.574 (1.3)	2.998 (1.1)	5.829 (2.0)	4.269 (1.5)	6.110 (2.1)	5.041 (1.8)	4.028 (1.5)	5.526 (2.0)
HBI	-.021 (0.5)	-.036 (0.9)	-.121 (2.2)	-.007 (0.2)			-.024 (0.6)		
BA79		.214 (5.7)	.142 (2.8)				.200 (5.2)	.217 (5.7)	.200 (5.3)
HBI*B79[a]			.151 (2.1)						
λ(EMP)				-.303 (2.4)	-.112 (1.1)	-.316 (2.5)	-.237 (1.9)		-.259 (2.1)
HBI[b]						-.068 (0.7)		-.159 (1.6)	-.121 (1.2)
$\bar{R}^2$	.129	.179	.184	.137	.130	.139	.183	.182	.187
N	541	541	541	541	541	541	541	541	541

Note: See footnotes to Tables 4.2, 4.7, and 4.8 for variables included in the model.
[a]The product of HBI and BA79.
[b]Instrumental variable estimate of HBI.

of attendance at an HBI on earnings in percentage terms was the direct effect $(-.131)$ plus the indirect effect $(.200)(.215)$ or $-.088$.

Finally, column 3 reports the results of allowing the effects of attendance at an HBI on earnings to vary with whether the individual actually graduated by 1979. The pattern of coefficients suggests that, holding other variables constant, individuals who had not graduated from HBIs earned less than individuals who had not graduated from other institutions. In contrast, other things held constant, graduates of HBIs earned more than graduates of other institutions. There may have been a larger payoff to attending an HBI, but only if the student succeeded in graduating. The lower earnings for nongraduates who attended HBIs undoubtedly reflects either perceptions that their quality, or the quality of the education they have received, is lower than that for nongraduates of other institutions, or simply increased discrimination against them.

EARLY CAREER OCCUPATIONAL PRESTIGE

Tables 4.11, 4.12, and 4.13 replicate the analyses of the previous three tables but replace the logarithm of hourly earnings with the index of occupational prestige in the occupation in which the individual was employed in 1979. The rationale for using this alternative variable is that individuals may trade off earnings early in their careers for training opportunities. Thus, occupational prestige may be a better measure of early career success than is earnings.

The results obtained when this alternative success measure is used are very similar to the earnings results, although neither correction for sample selection bias due to the nonrandom nature of employment status nor correction for attendance at an HBI mattered here. Once again, the analyses conducted for the pooled sample (Table 4.13) suggest that attendance at an HBI did not lead to an increase in black students' early career occupational success.[20]

ENROLLMENT IN GRADUATE EDUCATION

Historically, HBIs graduated many of the black Americans who went on to graduate and professional schools and who ultimately assumed professional positions in the black community. We discuss the role HBIs play in the production of black doctorates in the next section. Here, we examine the probability, conditional on having received a bachelor's degree by 1979, that graduates of HBIs in our sample were enrolled in a master's, doctoral, or professional degree program by 1979.

Table 4.11. 1979 Occupational Status Equations: Non-HBI Students
(Absolute Value of t Statistic)

	OLS				Selectivity Corrected	
	(1)	(2)	(3)	(4)	(1B)	(3B)
MALE	-.891 (0.4)	-1.301 (0.6)	.895 (0.5)	.520 (0.6)	-.607 (0.2)	.678 (0.3)
SAT	.291 (3.5)	.267 (3.0)	.214 (2.8)	.209 (2.6)	.273 (3.1)	.190 (2.2)
HSRANK	-8.358 (1.8)	-7.647 (1.6)	-2.636 (0.6)	-1.756 (0.4)	-8.319 (1.8)	-1.910 (0.4)
URBHS	2.635 (1.1)	2.790 (1.2)	3.126 (1.5)	3.079 (1.4)	2.310 (1.0)	2.778 (1.3)
MOMBA	2.397 (0.7)	2.626 (0.7)	.250 (0.1)	.250 (0.1)	2.221 (0.6)	.291 (0.1)
DADBA	5.189 (1.2)	5.523 (1.3)	6.046 (1.6)	6.350 (1.7)	5.479 (1.2)	6.994 (1.7)
DADSEI	.116 (1.5)	.111 (1.5)	.055 (0.8)	.058 (0.8)	.126 (1.7)	.065 (1.0)
PARINC	.001 (0.0)	-.006 (0.3)	.011 (0.5)	.003 (0.1)	-.002 (0.1)	.000 (0.0)
UNEMP	-13.382 (0.1)	-17.946 (0.2)	9.464 (0.1)	7.478 (0.1)	-.541 (0.0)	5.245 (0.1)
CSAT		.144 (1.0)		.147 (1.1)		
PRIV		.866 (0.3)		-.007 (0.0)		
BFACC		49.009 (1.1)		55.166 (1.5)		
BSTUDC		-28.715 (2.0)		-23.847 (1.8)		
EXPST		-.055 (0.8)		-.076 (0.6)		
BA79			15.083 (7.9)	14.936 (7.7)		15.199 (7.7)
λ(HBI)					2.934 (0.9)	2.777 (0.9)
λ(EMP)					-.826 (0.1)	1.902 (0.3)
$\overline{R}^2$	.129	.134	.290	.293	.125	.290
N	288	288	288	288	288	288

Note: Also included in each equation are dichotomous variables for the nonreporting of SAT; high school rank; urban high school; mother's and father's education levels; father's occupational status; parents' family income; and, where relevant, the proportion of black faculty.

Table 4.12. 1979 Occupational Status Equations: HBI Students
(Absolute Value of t Statistic)

	OLS				Selectivity Corrected	
	(1)	(2)	(3)	(4)	(1B)	(3B)
MALE	-3.998 (1.8)	-3.750 (1.7)	-4.417 (2.1)	-4.175 (2.1)	-3.196 (1.4)	-3.476 (1.8)
SAT	.051 (0.5)	.033 (0.3)	.016 (0.2)	-.012 (0.1)	.012 (0.1)	-.047 (0.5)
HSRANK	-16.383 (3.4)	-16.057 (3.3)	-11.212 (2.6)	-10.731 (2.4)	-16.154 (3.3)	-11.302 (3.6)
URBHS	-4.619 (1.7)	-4.266 (1.6)	-3.516 (1.5)	-3.204 (1.3)	-4.387 (1.6)	-3.599 (1.5)
MOMBA	-1.087 (0.2)	-.967 (0.2)	-3.556 (1.0)	-3.337 (1.0)	-2.303 (0.6)	-3.961 (1.1)
DADBA	-4.475 (1.0)	-5.060 (1.1)	-2.987 (0.7)	-3.578 (0.9)	-5.661 (1.3)	-3.772 (0.9)
DADSEI	.052 (0.7)	.069 (1.0)	.061 (1.0)	.071 (1.1)	.065 (0.9)	.075 (1.2)
PARINC	.087 (3.4)	.082 (3.0)	.072 (3.0)	.063 (2.7)	.089 (3.3)	.068 (2.9)
UNEMP	146.892 (1.4)	134.510 (1.2)	40.018 (0.4)	6.955 (0.0)	205.719 (1.9)	75.181 (0.8)
CSAT		-.206 (1.2)		-.141 (0.9)		
PRIV		2.834 (1.0)		1.123 (0.5)		
BFACC		.460 (0.0)		7.120 (0.1)		
BSTUDC		-11.168 (1.0)		-10.228 (1.0)		
EXPST		.093 (0.8)		.145 (1.4)		
BA79			15.205 (7.9)	15.196 (7.8)		15.130 (7.7)
λ(HBI)					2.590 (0.8)	4.249 (1.5)
λ(EMP)					-9.970 (1.5)	-4.527 (0.7)
R̄²	.116	.113	.297	.296	.119	.299
N	253	253	253	253	253	253

Note: See footnote to Table 4.11 for the other variables included in the model.

Table 4.13. 1979 Occupational Status Equations: All Students
(Absolute Value of t Statistic)

	OLS					Selectivity Corrected		
	(1)	(2)	(1A)	(1B)	(1C)	(2A)	(2B)	(2C)
MALE	-2.762 (1.8)	-1.836 (1.3)	-2.534 (1.6)	-2.595 (1.7)	-2.385 (1.5)	-1.899 (1.5)	-1.490 (1.1)	-1.515 (1.1)
SAT	.231 (3.6)	.166 (2.9)	.235 (3.7)	.212 (3.2)	.220 (3.3)	.164 (2.9)	.127 (2.1)	.126 (2.0)
HSRANK	-12.293 (3.7)	-6.706 (2.2)	-12.080 (3.6)	-12.363 (2.5)	-12.133 (3.6)	-6.740 (2.2)	-6.731 (2.2)	-6.778 (2.2)
URBHS	-.032 (0.0)	.646 (0.4)	.178 (0.1)	-.138 (0.1)	.036 (0.8)	.608 (0.4)	.313 (0.2)	.293 (0.2)
MOMBA	.761 (0.2)	-1.597 (0.7)	.405 (0.1)	.798 (0.3)	.409 (0.2)	-1.504 (0.6)	-1.584 (0.7)	-1.540 (0.6)
DADBA	-.754 (0.3)	.311 (0.1)	-1.253 (0.4)	-.646 (0.2)	-1.177 (0.4)	.461 (0.2)	.558 (0.2)	.628 (0.2)
DADSEI	.100 (1.9)	.069 (1.5)	.103 (2.0)	.105 (2.0)	.108 (2.1)	.068 (1.5)	.079 (1.7)	.078 (1.7)
PARINC	.036 (2.0)	.034 (2.3)	.037 (2.2)	.033 (2.0)	.035 (2.0)	.034 (2.2)	.030 (2.0)	.030 (1.9)
UNEMP	61.374 (0.9)	24.785 (0.4)	84.955 (1.1)	65.543 (0.9)	89.456 (1.2)	17.087 (0.2)	36.016 (0.6)	32.931 (0.5)
HBI	-.602 (0.4)	-2.016 (1.6)	-.433 (0.3)			-2.071 (1.6)		
BA79		15.175 (11.2)				15.246 (11.0)	15.367 (11.3)	15.400 (11.2)
λ(EMP)			-3.924 (0.9)		-4.148 (0.9)	1.141 (0.3)		.528 (0.1)
HBI[a]				-3.274 (1.0)	-2.736 (0.8)		-7.415 (2.2)	-7.489 (2.4)
$\bar{R}^2$	.109	.281	.109	.111	.110	.279	.286	.284
N	541	541	541	541	541	541	541	541

Note: See footnote to Table 4.11 for the other variables included in the model.
[a]Instrumental variable estimate of HBI.

In the aggregate, 33 percent of the individuals who received a bachelor's degree by 1979 were enrolled in such programs by 1979. The comparable percentages for graduates of HBIs was 27 and for graduates of other institutions 38. These raw percentages, however, ignore differences in the two groups in students' academic ability or family backgrounds (e.g., income), both of which might influence their propensities to attend graduate or professional school.

Table 4.14 presents estimates of probit probabilities of enrollment in graduate programs by 1979, conditional on having received a bachelor's degree. The simplest model (column 1) included measures of a student's academic ability at the time he or she graduated from high school, the student's family background at that time, and whether the student attended an HBI. A student's academic ability and parents' income both positively influenced the probability of having been enrolled in postgraduate education, but attendance at an HBI per se did not significantly increase this probability. Use of an instrument for attendance at an HBI, to control for its nonrandom nature (column 2), did not change any of these findings.

When the data were stratified by whether the students attended an HBI, the characteristics of the institutions the students attended can be entered into the models. This is done is columns 4 (non-HBIs) and 6 (HBIs). In each case, an increase in the proportion of black students in the institution's undergraduate student body is associated with an increase in the probability of enrollment in graduate education.

DID ATTENDANCE AT AN HBI MATTER?

Table 4.15 summarizes the predicted mean (across individuals) proportional differential impacts of enrollment in an HBI on the probability of having received a bachelor's degree by 1979, on hourly earnings (if employed) in 1979, and on the occupational prestige index (if employed) in 1979.

In addition to the single-equation (pooled sample) estimates that have already been discussed, estimates are presented for when separate "outcome equations" were estimated for individuals attending HBIs and other institutions. In these latter cases, estimates of mean differentials are reported for individuals initially in each sector. In addition, to ascertain the sensitivity of the findings to the statistical model used, estimates are reported for models in which attendance at an HBI was treated as exogenous, attendance at an HBI was treated as endogenous, and (where relevant) being employed was treated as endogenous. In each

Table 4.14. Probit Probability of Enrollment in Graduate Programs by 1979 (Absolute Value of t Statistic)

	All		Non-HBI		HBI	
	(1)	(2)	(3)	(4)	(5)	(6)
MALE	.046 (0.2)	.027 (0.2)	.112 (0.5)	.094 (0.4)	.106 (0.4)	.178 (0.7)
SAT	.011 (1.8)	.013 (2.0)	.009 (1.0)	.004 (0.5)	-.011 (1.0)	.011 (0.9)
HSRANK	-.713 (1.5)	-.694 (2.0)	-.142 (0.3)	-.064 (0.1)	-2.059 (3.1)	-2.042 (3.0)
MOMBA	.278 (1.0)	.273 (1.0)	.463 (1.4)	.289 (0.8)	.030 (0.6)	-.044 (0.1)
DADBA	-.569 (1.6)	-.559 (1.6)	-.059 (0.1)	-.050 (0.1)	-2.273 (2.6)	-2.290 (2.5)
DADSEI	.003 (0.6)	.003 (0.6)	.002 (0.3)	.002 (0.3)	.004 (0.6)	.006 (0.5)
PARINC	.003 (2.1)	.003 (2.1)	.002 (1.0)	.003 (1.1)	.007 (2.4)	.007 (2.2)
HBI	-.194 (1.3)					
HBI[a]		.047 (0.1)				
CSAT				.017 (1.1)		-.015 (0.8)
PRIV				-.044 (0.2)		-.231 (0.7)
BFACC				-4.747 (0.8)		-1.832 (1.6)
BSTUDC				3.547 (1.7)		4.914 (2.0)
EXPST				.003 (0.4)		.023 (1.5)
N	340	340	175	175	165	165
χ²/DOF	28.6 (14)	27.0 (14)	13.3 (13)	19.1 (19)	34.5 (13)	42.0 (19)

Note: Probit probabilities conditional on having received a bachelor's degree and enrollment in a master's, doctoral, or professional degree program. The proportions of college graduates enrolled in such programs were: All (340): .33; HBI: .27; Non-HBI: .38.
[a]Instrumental variable estimate of HBI.

Table 4.15. Predicted Mean Percentage Impacts of Enrollment in HBI (Standard Deviation of Impact across Individuals)

	BA79	
	HBI Exogenous	*HBI Endogenous*[a]
Single equation	.090 (.015)	.213 (.039)
Separate equation for each sector		
a) in HBIs	.288 (.385)	
b) not in HBIs	.255 (.334)	

	WAGE79		
		HBI Endogenous[a]	
	HBI Exogenous	*(N)*	*(Y)*
Single equation	−.021	−.107	−.066
Separate equation for each sector			
a) in HBIs	−.020 (.152)	−.302 (.135)	−.293 (.140)
b) not in HBIs	.020 (.173)	.045 (.188)	.050 (.197)

	SEI79		
		HBI Endogenous[a]	
	HBI Exogenous	*(N)*	*(Y)*
Single equation	−.013	−.073	−.061
Separate equation for each sector			
a) in HBIs	−.007 (.155)	−.090 (.140)	−.089 (.144)
b) not in HBIs	−.010 (.166)	−.089 (.164)	−.078 (.172)

Note: (N) = no sample selection correction for employment status; (Y) = sample selection correction for employment status—assumed to be independent of sample selection correction for sector choice.
[a]Endogenous dichotomous variable in the single equation, sample selection correction for institutional sector in the separate equation for each sector model.

case, the models used are those that excluded the vector of institutional characteristics and (for wages and occupational status) excluded receipt of a bachelor's degree by 1979. In each case, the predicted impact was computed for each individual in the sample and then the mean of the individual responses reported.[21]

Table 4.15 makes clear that attendance at an HBI substantially increased the probability that black students in the sample received a bachelor's degree by 1979. Depending on the specific model and statistical method used, the mean probability was between 9 and 29 percent higher if a student attended an HBI. In contrast, the impact of attendance at an HBI on early career labor market success, as measured by 1979 earnings or occupational prestige, was much smaller. In many cases the estimates were negative, although given the statistical insignificance of the underlying coefficients, all of these impacts on early career labor market success are probably insignificantly different from zero.

How could HBIs have improved black students' graduation probabilities but not improved their early career labor market success? At least two explanations come to mind. On the one hand, employers may have discriminated more against black graduates of HBIs than they did against black graduates of other institutions.[22] On the other hand, the quality of education received by black students and the graduation standards may have been lower at HBIs. The data we have used do not permit us to distinguish between these two explanations.[23]

THE PRODUCTION AND EARLY CAREER ATTAINMENT OF BLACK U.S. CITIZEN DOCTORATES

Historically, HBIs have provided many of the black college graduates who have gone on to earn doctoral degrees in the United States. In recent years, approximately 40 percent of the new doctorates granted to black citizens have gone to individuals who received their undergraduate degrees from HBIs, even though HBIs grant only about 30 percent of the bachelor's degrees received by black Americans. Thus, HBIs are asserted to be an important component of the pipeline for the production of black doctorates (U.S. House of Representatives 1991).

This section investigates the role of HBIs in the production of black doctorates, using special tabulations prepared for us by the National Research Council from the Survey of Earned Doctorates (SED). Each year when doctoral candidates submit their dissertations to their graduate schools and receive their degrees, they are asked to respond to the SED. Of primary interest to us here are their responses relating to their field of doctoral study, the institutions at which they received their undergraduate and graduate degrees, and their plans for future employment or study. Because of the small number of doctoral degrees granted to black citizens in any one year, most of the tabulations that follow are based on data from a recent five-year period.

Table 4.16 presents data on the share of doctorates granted by HBIs to black U.S. citizens and the share that went to individuals who received their undergraduate degrees from HBIs, by field, over the 1987–91 period. Focusing initially on the latter, the share of doctorates granted to black citizens with undergraduate degrees from HBIs was .39. However, this aggregate figure masks considerable variation across fields. Over 47 percent of all black citizens' doctorates granted during the period were in the field of education, and the share of education doctorates going to individuals with undergraduate degrees from HBIs was .48. While the

Table 4.16. Share of Black U.S. Citizen Doctorates by Field, 1987–91

Field	Total Doctorates Granted to Black U.S. Citizens	Share Granted by HBIs	Share Granted to Graduates of Undergraduate HBIs
Physical sciences	164	.10	.28
Engineering	125	.03	.21
Life sciences	382	.10	.36
Social sciences	330	.09	.27
Psychology	507	.08	.22
Humanities	383	.06	.33
Education	1,993	.09	.48
Professional/other	331	.13	.43
Total Doctorates	4,215	.09	.39

Source: Computed from special tabulations prepared by the Office of Scientific and Engineering Personnel, National Research Council from the Survey of Earned Doctorates (sponsored by five federal agencies—National Science Foundation, National Institute of Health, U.S. Department of Education, National Endowment for the Humanities, and the U.S. Department of Agriculture—and conducted by the National Research Council.)

analogous shares for the professional fields, the life sciences, and the humanities were all greater than .3, the shares in the physical sciences, the social sciences, engineering, and psychology were less than .3. In these latter fields, at least, undergraduates from HBIs are not overrepresented among new black doctorates.

This table also indicates that the share of doctorates granted by HBIs was .09 during the period. The number of HBIs that grant doctoral degrees in any year is actually very small. For example, as Table 4.17 indicates, in 1991 there were only eight such institutions, and over two-thirds of the total number of degrees they granted were by Howard and Clark Atlanta Universities alone. If one excludes doctorates granted in education, the number of HBIs producing doctorates falls to four. The small number of doctorates produced annually by many of the doctoral programs in HBIs leads to the concern that these programs may be too small to reach the critical mass necessary to efficiently train doctoral students (Bowen and Rudenstine 1992).

What types of graduate institutions do graduates of HBIs attend for doctoral study, and how do these compare to the institutional types that other black doctorates attend? This question is of some importance because, as we show below, where one attends graduate school heavily influences a new black doctorate's employment prospects. To answer this question, Table 4.18 presents cross-tabulations, by field, of black doctorates' undergraduate and graduate institutional types. The graduate institutions are broken down into HBIs, Research I doctorate-granting

Table 4.17. HBIs That Conferred Doctorates in 1991, by Major

Institution	Total	PS	EAM	MC	ENG	BIO	HEA	AGR	PSY	SOC	HUM	EDU	PROF
Howard	60	2			1	14	1		7	13	6	4	12
Clark Atlanta	74	2				4			3	9	3	44	9
Morgan State	3											3	
Univ. Maryland-Eastern Shore	2		1					1					
Jackson State	4											4	
South Carolina State	15											15	
Meharry Medical	4					4							
Texas Southern	26											26	
Total	188	4	1	0	1	22	1	1	10	22	9	96	2

Source: National Research Council, Doctorate Recipients from United States Universities: Summary Report 1990 (Washington, D.C.: National Academy Press, 1991), Appendix Table A7.

Note: Some of these doctorates went to other than black U.S. citizens. Abbreviations for majors are as follows: PS = Physical Sciences; EAM = Earth, Atmospheric, and Ocean Sciences; MC = Mathematics and Computer/Information Sciences; ENG = Engineering; BIO = Biology; HEA = Health; AGR = Agriculture; PSY = Psychology; SOC = Social Sciences; HUM = Humanities; EDU = Education; PROF = Professional.

Table 4.18. Number of Black U.S. Citizen Doctorates Granted, by Field and Type of Undergraduate and Doctoral Institution, 1987–91

	Undergrad. Inst.																
Field of Doctorate	Doctoral Inst.																
	All				HBIS				Liberal Arts I and Research I				Other				
	(T)	(H)	(R)	(O)	(T)	(H)	(R)	(O)	(T)	(H)	(R)	(O)	(T)	(H)	(R)	(O)	
Physical sciences	164	16 (.10)	87 (.53)	61 (.37)	46	11 (.24)	16 (.35)	19 (.41)	58	3 (.05)	44 (.76)	11 (.19)	60	2 (.03)	27 (.45)	31 (.52)	
Engineering	125	4 (.03)	86 (.69)	35 (.28)	26	2 (.08)	14 (.54)	10 (.39)	53	1 (.02)	49 (.92)	3 (.06)	46	1 (.02)	23 (.50)	22 (.48)	
Life sciences	382	37 (.10)	217 (.57)	128 (.34)	139	25 (.18)	66 (.48)	48 (.34)	91	2 (.02)	72 (.79)	17 (.19)	152	10 (.07)	79 (.52)	63 (.41)	
Social sciences	330	29 (.09)	173 (.52)	128 (.39)	88	14 (.16)	44 (.50)	30 (.34)	90	4 (.04)	62 (.69)	24 (.27)	152	11 (.07)	67 (.44)	74 (.49)	
Psychology	507	41 (.08)	238 (.47)	228 (.45)	114	22 (.19)	47 (.41)	45 (.40)	189	9 (.05)	114 (.60)	66 (.35)	204	10 (.05)	77 (.38)	117 (.58)	
Humanities	383	22 (.06)	223 (.58)	138 (.36)	128	15 (.12)	57 (.45)	56 (.44)	112	3 (.03)	83 (.74)	26 (.23)	143	4 (.03)	83 (.58)	56 (.39)	
Education	1,993	177 (.09)	705 (.35)	1,111 (.56)	955	146 (.15)	296 (.31)	513 (.54)	238	3 (.01)	135 (.57)	100 (.42)	800	28 (.04)	274 (.34)	498 (.62)	
Professional/other	331	42 (.13)	155 (.47)	134 (.40)	141	30 (.21)	56 (.40)	55 (.39)	70	3 (.04)	39 (.56)	28 (.40)	120	9 (.08)	60 (.50)	51 (.42)	
Total doctorates	4,215	368 (.09)	1,884 (.45)	1,963 (.47)	1,637	265 (.16)	596 (.36)	776 (.47)	901	28 (.03)	598 (.66)	275 (.31)	1,677	75 (.05)	690 (.41)	912 (.54)	

Source: Special tabulations prepared by the Office of Scientific and Engineering Personnel, National Research Council from the Survey of Earned Doctorates (sponsored by five federal agencies—National Science Foundation, National Institute of Health, U.S. Department of Education, National Endowment for the Humanities, and the U.S. Department of Agriculture—and conducted by the National Research Council).

Note: Figures in parentheses represent share of doctorates in the field/undergraduate institution category from the graduate institution category. Column subheads are as follows: (T) = all doctorate granting-institutions; (H) = historically black institutions that grant doctorates; (R) = Research I doctorate-granting institutions; (O) = all other doctorate-granting institutions.

institutions (the institutions that produce a large number of doctorates in a number of fields and whose doctoral programs are often highly rated), and other institutions.[24] The undergraduate institutions are broken down into HBIs, Liberal Arts I (selective liberal arts) and Research I institutions, and other institutions.

In the aggregate, 9 percent of black doctorates during the 1987–91 period were granted by HBIs, 45 percent were granted by Research I institutions, and 47 percent were granted by other institutions. For those black doctorates whose undergraduate degrees were earned at HBIs, the comparable figures were 16, 36, and 47 percent, respectively; while for black doctorates from Liberal Arts I and Research I undergraduate institutions, the figures were 3, 66, and 31 percent, respectively. That is, black doctorates who earned undergraduate degrees at HBIs were much more likely to attend HBIs, and somewhat less likely to attend Research I institutions, for their doctoral study. Perusal of the field-specific data suggests that the same pattern holds for each of the doctoral fields, although in some cases the differences are not as large as the overall ones.

Why do black doctorates who received their undergraduate degrees from HBIs tend to be less likely to attend elite Research I doctoral programs than are graduates from Liberal Arts I and Research I institutions? In part, this tendency may reflect differences in the ability levels and undergraduate training of students from HBIs vis-à-vis their counterparts from research and liberal arts institutions. In part, it may reflect their personal preferences to remain for graduate study in what they perceive to be a supportive environment. And, in part, it may reflect ignorance about HBIs, discriminatory attitudes toward the graduates of HBIs, or the failure of faculty in the elite graduate programs to aggressively recruit potential graduate students from HBIs, most of which are located in different areas of the country than are the elite graduate programs.

The SED data do not permit one to distinguish between these various hypotheses. However, the facts that average test scores of black students tend to be lower at HBIs than at other institutions (see, e.g., Table 4.2) and that over a recent seven-year period only 20 percent of National Science Foundation Black Minority Graduate Fellowship winners received their undergraduate degrees at HBIs (Table 4.19) suggest that perceptions of differential ability or training are at least part of the problem. Indeed, 67 percent of these fellowship winners from HBIs came from four institutions, and 45 percent came from Howard University alone. The perceived quality of HBIs and their students may fall off quite rapidly.

Table 4.19. National Science Foundation Black Minority Graduate Fellowship Winners

Year	Number of Black Winners	Number of Black Winners from HBIs	Share of Black Winners from HBIs
1992	42	8	.191
1991	59	17	.288
1990	52	13	.250
1989	27	5	.185
1988	23	1	.044
1987	16	3	.188
1986	17	1	.059
1985	19	3	.158
Total 1985–92	255	51	.200

Source: Calculations from National Science Foundation, "Outstanding Science Students Awarded NSF Minority Graduate Fellowships" (Washington, D.C.: National Science Foundation): NSF PR 92–26, 91–23, 90–22, 89–18, 88–14, 87–16, 86–19, and 85–19).

The final information in the SED that is useful to us comes from the question that asks doctorates at the time their dissertations are approved if they have already made definite employment plans. For those who have, additional questions are asked about whether academic employment, another form of employment, or a postdoctoral appointment has been obtained. Finally, for those entering academic appointments, the name of the academic institution at which they will be employed is reported.

The tabulations reported in Table 4.20 indicate that, in the aggregate, 69 percent of all black U.S. citizen new doctorates during the 1987–91 period had definite employment plans at the time that they received their degrees and that 58 percent of these had definite plans to work in academia or in postdoctoral positions. The comparable percentages are both higher for doctorates from Research I institutions than they are for doctorates from HBIs; however, once one breaks the data down by field, a consistent pattern of results does not emerge. That is, once one controls for field, on balance doctorates from HBIs are roughly equally likely to have definite plans at the time they receive their degrees and equally likely to have a postdoctoral or an academic position as are doctorates from Research I institutions.

What is different, though, is the type of academic position doctorates receive if they do enter the academic sector. Table 4.21 provides data on the shares of black U.S. citizen new doctorates with definite plans in the academic sector who go on to employment in HBIs (including Howard University), Research I or Liberal Arts I institutions, and other institu-

Table 4.20. Black U.S. Citizen Doctorates, 1987–91

	All Inst.	Type of Doctoral Inst.			Type of Undergraduate Inst.		
		HBI	Research I	Other	HBI	Research I or Liberal Arts I	Other
All fields							
Total number	4,233	369	1,890	1,974	1,637	901	1,677
Share with definite plans	.69	.63	.71	.69	.71	.69	.68
Share of those with definite plans going to postdocs or academia	.58	.50	.65	.54	.55	.64	.60
Physical sciences							
Total number	164	116	87	61	46	58	60
Share with definite plans	.72	.44	.78	.70	.72	.71	.73
Share of those with definite plans going to postdocs or academia	.52	.72	.50	.53	.45	.53	.57
Engineering							
Total number	126	4	86	36	26	53	46
Share with definite plans	.67	.75	.71	.56	.65	.66	.70
Share of those with definite plans going to postdocs or academia	.51	.67	.54	.40	.35	.48	.61
Life sciences							
Total number	384	37	219	128	139	91	152
Share with definite plans	.71	.76	.71	.70	.72	.77	.68
Share of those with definite plans going to postdocs or academia	.80	.85	.78	.82	.84	.80	.76

Social sciences							
Total number	332	29	175	128	88	90	152
Share with definite plans	.63	.62	.65	.60	.68	.63	.59
Share of those with definite plans going to postdocs or academia	.73	.67	.76	.70	.75	.58	.80
Psychology							
Total number	507	41	238	228	114	189	204
Share with definite plans	.69	.54	.68	.72	.73	.62	.73
Share of those with definite plans going to postdocs or academia	.49	.41	.57	.44	.48	.53	.48
Humanities							
Total number	385	22	224	139	128	112	143
Share with definite plans	.74	.86	.72	.74	.81	.75	.67
Share of those with definite plans going to postdocs or academia	.91	.89	.90	.94	.91	.98	.86
Education							
Total number	2,002	177	706	1,119	995	238	800
Share with definite plans	.69	.60	.71	.69	.70	.72	.67
Share of those with definite plans going to postdocs or academia	.46	.26	.52	.46	.43	.51	.50

Source: Special tabulations prepared by the National Research Council's Office of Scientific and Engineering Personnel from the Survey of Earned Doctorates.

Table 4.21. Black U.S. Citizen New Doctorates, 1987–91, with Definite Plans in the Academic Sector

Share Going to Employment in:	All Inst.	Type of Doctoral Inst.			Type of Undergraduate Inst.		
		HBI	Research I	Other	HBI	Research I or Liberal Arts I	Other
All Fields							
HBIs	.23	.58	.18	.25	.41	.12	.12
RI/LAI inst.	.21	.04	.31	.13	.14	.36	.21
Other U.S. inst.	.56	.44	.51	.62	.46	.52	.67
Physical sciences							
HBIs	.32	.67	.27	.31	.67	.25	.10
RI/LAI inst.	.26	.00	.40	.15	.11	.50	.10
Other U.S. inst.	.42	.33	.33	.54	.22	.25	.80
Engineering							
HBIs	.30	1.00	.17	.57	.80	.18	.24
RI/LAI inst.	.27	.00	.38	.00	.00	.36	.29
Other U.S. inst.	.42	.00	.46	.43	.20	.45	.47
Life sciences							
HBIs	.34	.55	.23	.43	.62	.04	.18
RI/LAI inst.	.18	.09	.30	.05	.11	.30	.18
Other U.S. inst.	.48	.36	.47	.52	.28	.65	.63

Social sciences							
HBIs	.17	.40	.12	.21	.32	.12	.11
RI/LAI inst.	.25	.00	.35	.17	.16	.35	.25
Other U.S. inst.	.57	.60	.54	.63	.51	.54	.63
Psychology							
HBIs	.12	.80	.14	.04	.23	.13	.05
RI/LAI inst.	.31	.00	.32	.33	.26	.34	.31
Other U.S. inst.	.57	.20	.55	.64	.52	.53	.64
Humanities							
HBIs	.21	.63	.16	.25	.32	.16	.13
RI/LAI inst.	.28	.00	.34	.22	.11	.47	.28
Other U.S. inst.	.51	.38	.50	.53	.57	.37	.59
Education							
HBIs	.24	.40	.21	.25	.40	.08	.12
RI/LA I inst.	.15	.00	.27	.08	.12	.28	.14
Other U.S. inst.	.61	.60	.53	.68	.48	.64	.74

Source: Special tabulations prepared by the National Research Council's Office of Scientific and Engineering Personnel from the Survey of Earned Doctorates.

tions. In the aggregate, these shares are .23, .21, and .56, respectively. However, new doctorates from HBIs are much more likely to be employed in HBIs and much less likely to be employed in Research I or Liberal Arts I institutions than are new doctorates from Research I institutions.[25] Similarly, new doctorates whose undergraduate degrees were from HBIs are much more likely to be employed in HBIs and much less likely to be employed in Research I or Liberal Arts I institutions than are new doctorates whose undergraduate degrees came from Research I or Liberal Arts I institutions.[26] Similar results hold for each of the seven specific fields for which data are tabulated in Table 4.21.

Again, one cannot ascertain if the sorting by institution type that occurs in these data is due to inherent differences in the ability or training of black doctorates who attended HBIs as undergraduate or doctoral students vis-à-vis their counterparts at Research I or Liberal Arts I institutions, to lack of information about and effort to recruit students from HBIs by the Liberal Arts I and Research I institutions, or to discriminatory preferences. If, however, a social goal is to increase the flow of talented black students into Ph.D. programs and ultimately into academic positions in elite teaching and research institutions, a number of actions are possible.

First, one could increase the number and size of doctoral programs in HBIs.[27] Second, one could more aggressively recruit graduates of HBIs into the doctoral programs of Research I institutions and pursue extra efforts to retain these students until graduation. Third, one could more aggressively recruit black students who otherwise would attend HBIs to attend undergraduate programs at Research I or Liberal Arts I institutions. The data we have analyzed do not permit one to conclude which option is best. However, the third option is likely to have adverse effects on the "better" undergraduate HBIs, and, without other policies, the first option appears likely to continue the current segmentation of black doctorate employment. Hence, building "pipelines" between the HBIs' undergraduate programs and the Research I institutions' doctoral programs may well be the preferred strategy.

CONCLUDING REMARKS

What should public policy be toward the Historically Black Institutions of higher education? In an increasingly multicultural society, should public policy encourage the integration and/or incorporation of HBIs into the larger and often better funded historically white institutions? Or should public policy facilitate the HBIs "specializing" in the education of blacks and other underrepresented minorities on American campuses, by providing the HBIs with improved facilities and increased annual support?

At the outset, it should be stressed that the only real question relates to the status of public HBIs. There is a long tradition in American private education of institutions being established by particular religious groups and then continuing to draw the majority of their students from members of these groups. No one objects to Catholics voluntarily attending Notre Dame or Georgetown, Mormons voluntarily attending Brigham Young, or Jews voluntarily attending Yeshiva or Brandeis. If voluntary association with predominately members of one's own group in a private *nondiscriminating* institution is deemed by an individual to be in his or her best interest, this choice should be permitted. Hence, no one should question the importance to black Americans of the private HBIs, those institutions that receive much of their support through private fund-raising activities conducted by the United Negro College Fund.

What should public policy be toward the public HBIs? Our empirical analyses in the second section focused on all HBIs as a group; however, we did not find that the public/private distinction was an important predictor of the benefits of attendance at an HBI. For black students attending college in the early 1970s, attendance at an HBI did substantially enhance their probability of receiving a bachelor's degree within seven years. However, it had no apparent effect on their early career labor market success and on their probability of enrolling in postcollege graduate or professional schools. Moreover, for none of these outcomes did it appear that attendance at an HBI yielded larger benefits for students from low-income families or students with low test scores than it did for other black students.

Of course, "early success" is not the same as "career success," and in future work we will examine if data from later waves of the NLS72 provide any evidence of larger gains for students who attended HBIs.[28] In addition, all of our analyses were conditional upon students having enrolled in a four-year institution. We did not address whether the presence of HBIs enhances the probability that black students enroll in four-year institutions, and that too needs to be addressed in future research.

Furthermore, to contemplate making policy recommendations for the 1990s, up-to-date evidence is required on the effects of attendance at HBIs. Given that one needs data for at least seven to ten years after entrance to college to conduct any meaningful analyses, about the best one can do is to use data on students who entered college in the 1980s. In subsequent work, we will conduct such analyses using data from High School and Beyond, a national longitudinal survey of students who graduated from high school in 1980 and 1982.[29]

Our analyses of the National Research Council's Survey of Earned Doctorates provided evidence on the patterns of black doctorates in recent years with respect to their undergraduate institutions, their graduate institutions, and whether they achieved academic positions in major American liberal arts and research/doctoral institutions. To the extent that one wishes to get more black Americans into faculty positions at major American colleges and universities, our tabulations suggest the need to increase the flow of black students into doctoral programs in major research institutions.

This conclusion presumes that hiring practices at American universities will remain the same and that perceptions of the quality of students at lesser programs, as well as the quality of training they receive, will remain unchanged. If federal funding for doctoral programs at HBIs could lead to high-quality programs that attract high-quality students, such funding may provide a viable option. Given the likely small scale of these programs and the complementary resources (e.g., libraries, faculty quality in other closely related fields) that they will have available (or unavailable) to them, one must question whether this option makes sense. Building better pipelines between the undergraduate HBIs and the Research I institutions' doctoral programs appears to be a preferred strategy.

Of course, increasing the flow of black Americans into faculty positions at major American colleges and universities is not an objective shared by all. Many people are justifiably concerned with simply increasing the production of black Ph.D.s, regardless of where they are ultimately employed. None of the research that we conducted in the third section really bears on methods to accomplish this objective, and this too is a subject for future research.

FORMAL STATISTICAL MODELS USED IN THE ANALYSES

THE DECISION TO ATTEND AN HBI

The decision to attend an HBI can be modeled as:

$$I^*_{1i} = Z_i\gamma_1 + u_{1i}$$
$$I_{1i} = 1 \text{ if } I^*_{1i} > 0$$
$$I_{1i} = 0 \text{ if } I^*_{1i} \leq 0. \tag{4.1}$$

Here I^*_1 is an unobservable variable indicating desire to attend an HBI, Z is a vector of covariates that influence the probability of attending an HBI, γ_1 is a vector of coefficients, and u_1 is a normally distributed disturbance term with mean 0 and variance σ_{11}. While we cannot observe the value of I^*_1, without loss of generality the individual is assumed to enroll in an HBI ($I_1 = 1$) if the value of I^*_1 is greater than zero and not to enroll in an HBI ($I_1 = 0$) otherwise. Under these assumptions, equation 4.2 describes the probit model that was used to estimate the choice of college sector, where Φ is the standard normal distribution function:

$$P(I_{1i} = 1|Z_i) = \Phi(Z_i\gamma_1/\sigma_1). \tag{4.2}$$

BACHELOR'S DEGREE ATTAINMENT

Separate equations, by sector, were estimated for whether an individual attained a bachelor's degree by 1979. We assumed that:

$$BA79^*_{Hi} = B_i\gamma_H + W_{Hi}\alpha_H + v_{Hi}$$
$$BA79_{Hi} = 1 \text{ if } BA79^*_{Hi} > 0$$
$$BA79_{Hi} = 0 \text{ if } BA79^*_{Hi} \leq 0 \tag{4.3}$$

$$BA79^*_{Oi} = B_i\gamma_O + W_{Oi}\alpha_O + v_{Oi}$$
$$BA79_{Oi} = 1 \text{ if } BA79^*_{Oi} > 0$$
$$BA79_{Oi} = 0 \text{ if } BA79^*_{Oi} \leq 0. \tag{4.4}$$

Here $BA79^*$ is an unobservable variable indicating desire to attain a bachelor's degree. Without loss of generality, the individual is assumed to have attained a bachelor's degree by 1979 ($BA79 = 1$) if $BA79^*$ is greater than zero and not to have a degree ($BA79 = 0$) otherwise. B is a set of explanatory variables describing individual and family background characteristics, and W is a vector of variables describing college character-istics that one might expect to influence bachelor's degree attainment. Assuming that v_H and v_O are normally distributed disturbance terms with zero means, equations 4.3 and 4.4 can be estimated by probit maximum likelihood.[30] Equation 4.3 is estimated using the subsample that attended HBIs and 4.4 using the subsample that did not attend HBIs.

In order to compute the average percentage differential of whether an individual would have been more likely to achieve a bachelor's degree had he or she attended an HBI, probit coefficient estimates were used from equations 4.3 and 4.4 to construct predicted values $\widehat{BA79}_H$ and $\widehat{BA79}_O$ for each individual. The predicted percentage differential for each individual was calculated as:

$$(\widehat{BA79}_H/\widehat{BA79}_O) - 1. \tag{4.5}$$

The predicted percentage differential was then averaged across individuals, by sector.

Bachelor's degree attainment equations, using data pooled across individuals in both sectors, were also estimated, treating HBI first as exogenous and then as endogenous:

$$\begin{aligned}
BA79^*_{Bi} &= B_I\gamma_B + \delta_B I_{1i} + v_{Bi} \\
BA79_{Bi} &= 1 \text{ if } BA79^*_{Bi} > 0 \\
BA79_{Bi} &= 0 \text{ if } BA79^*_{Bi} \leq 0.
\end{aligned} \tag{4.6}$$

Assuming that v_B is a normally distributed disturbance term with mean zero and variance σ_{BB}, equation 4.6 can be estimated as a probit using maximum likelihood. In order to treat HBI as endogenous, an instrument for it, I_1, was obtained through estimation of equation 4.2, which is described in the first section of this appendix.

The difference in the probability of receiving a bachelor's degree by 1979 if an individual attended an HBI was computed for each individual in the sample, and the individual differences were then averaged:

$$(1/N)\Sigma[\Phi(\{B_i\hat{\gamma}_B + \hat{\delta}_B\}/\hat{\sigma}_B) - \Phi(\{B_i\hat{\gamma}_B\}/\hat{\sigma}_B)]. \tag{4.7}$$

Here Σ indicates summation over all of the individuals in the pooled sample; the coefficient δ_B was estimated first treating attendance at an HBI as exogenous and then using the instrumental variable estimate.

WAGE EQUATIONS

Hourly wage equations for individuals in each sector (HBI, non-HBI) were first separately estimated. Let $LNWAGE^*_{Hi}$ be the hourly wage rate received if an individual attended an HBI and $LNWAGE^*_{Oi}$ be that value if he or she attended an other (non-HBI) college.[31] The following equations were assumed:

$$LNWAGE*_{Hi} = X_i\beta_H + W_{Hi}\omega_H + u_{Hi} \qquad (4.8)$$

$$LNWAGE*_{Oi} = X_i\beta_O + W_{Oi}\omega_O + u_{Oi}. \qquad (4.9)$$

Here X is a set of individual, family, and background explanatory variables that might influence wage rate, W is a vector of college characteristics, and u_H and u_O are mean zero, normally distributed disturbance terms with variances σ_{HH} and σ_{OO}.

Because individuals may systematically self-select into an HBI or a non-HBI (based on tastes, constraints, etc.), estimation of equations 4.8 and 4.9 on data from each sector separately, without taking into account the college sector choice decision, may result in biased estimates of the coefficients. Thus, the choice of sector must be added to the model. The choice equation of whether to attend an HBI was described by equations 4.1 and 4.2; 4.2 was estimated by maximum likelihood techniques.

For any individual in the sample, realizations of $LNWAGE*_H$ and $LNWAGE*_O$ will not both be observed. If $I_1 = 1$, then $LNWAGE_H = LNWAGE*_H$; if $I_1 = 0$, then $LNWAGE_H$ is not observed. If $I_1 = 0$, then $LNWAGE_O = LNWAGE*_O$; if $I_1 = 1$, then $LNWAGE_O$ is not observed. The conditional (on college sector choice) expectations of equations 4.8 and 4.9 are:

$$
\begin{aligned}
E(LNWAGE_{Hi}|X_i,W_{Hi}) &= E(LNWAGE*_{Hi}|X_i, W_{Hi}, I_{1i} = 1) \\
&= X_i\beta_H + W_{Hi}\omega_H + E(u_{Hi}|I_{1i} = 1) \\
&= X_i\beta_H + W_{Hi}\omega_H + (\sigma_{H1}/\sigma_1)[\phi(Z_i\gamma_1/\sigma_1)/\Phi(Z_i\gamma_1/\sigma_1)]
\end{aligned} \qquad (4.10)
$$

$$
\begin{aligned}
E(LNWAGE_{Oi}|X_i,W_{Oi}) &= E(LNWAGE*_{Oi}|X_i, W_{Oi}, I_{1i} = 0) \\
&= X_i\beta_O + W_{Oi}\omega_O + E(u_{Oi}|I_{1i} = 0) \\
&= X_i\beta_O + W_{Oi}\omega_O - (\sigma_{O1}/\sigma_1)[\phi(Z_i\gamma_1/\sigma_1)/(1 - \Phi(Z_i\gamma_1/\sigma_1))]
\end{aligned} \qquad (4.11)
$$

where ϕ is the standard normal density function, $\sigma_{H1} = \text{cov}(u_H, u_1)$, and $\sigma_{O1} = \text{cov}(u_O, u_1)$.

Heckman (1979) describes a method to estimate consistently the coefficients described in equations 4.10 and 4.11. Equation 4.2, the college sector choice probit, can be estimated on the entire sample using maximum likelihood. Utilizing estimates of γ_1 and each individual's characteristics, the inverse of Mills' ratio (λ_H or λ_O) can be calculated for each observation in the sample, where $\lambda_H = [\phi(Z\gamma_1/\sigma_1)/\Phi(Z\gamma_1/\sigma_1)]$ and $\lambda_o = - [\phi(Z\gamma_1/\sigma_1)/(1-\Phi(Z\gamma_1/\sigma_1))]$. Then the predicted inverse Mills' ratio can be added as an explanatory variable to the wage equations. The coefficients of the explanatory variables can then be consistently estimated when OLS is applied to the augmented equations:

$$LNWAGE_{Hi} = X_i\beta_H + W_{Hi}\omega_H + \theta_H\hat{\lambda}_{Hi} + v_{Hi} \tag{4.12}$$

$$LNWAGE_{Oi} = X_i\beta_O + W_{Oi}\omega_O + \theta_O\hat{\lambda}_{Oi} + V_{Oi} \tag{4.13}$$

where $\theta_H = \sigma_{H1}/\sigma_1$ and $\theta_O = \sigma_{O1}/\sigma_1$.[32] Equation 4.12 was estimated for the subsample that attended HBIs, and 4.13 for the subsample that attended non-HBIs.

One problem with the above analysis is that not all of the individuals in the sample are employed.[33] The switching regression model with more than one decision function is described by Maddala (1983). The two decisions—HBI versus other (non-HBI) college attendance and employment—fall under what Maddala terms a "joint model"; all four outcomes can be observed in the sample.[34] Thus the decisions are defined over all of the observations in the sample. The following (reduced-form) employment equation can be added to the above model:

$$I^*_{2i} = N_i\gamma_2 + u_{2i}$$
$$I_{2i} = 1 \text{ if } I^*_{2i} > 0$$
$$I_{2i} = 0 \text{ if } I^*_{2i} \leq 0. \tag{4.14}$$

I^*_2 is an observable variable indicating desire to be employed, N is a set of covariates (including nonlabor income, number of children, and state unemployment rate) that influences individuals' employment outcomes, and u_2 is a normally distributed disturbance term with mean zero. While we cannot observe the value of I^*_2, the individual is assumed to be employed ($I_2 = 1$) if the value of I^*_2 is greater than zero and not to be employed ($I_2 = 0$) otherwise. If it is assumed that $\text{cov}(u_2, u_1) = 0$, then equation 4.14 can be estimated as a probit on the entire sample, the inverse of Mills' ratio calculated for those who are employed, and then the ratio added to equations 4.12 and 4.13.[35]

Next, to compute the average percentage hourly wage differential between attendance at an HBI versus other college attendance, coefficients from equations 4.12 and 4.13 were used to construct predicted values of $LNWAGE_H$ and $LNWAGE_O$ for each individual. More specifically, for a random individual who went to college in a certain sector and was employed in 1979, we ask what were his or her expected earnings in the HBI sector and what were they in the non-HBI sector. Thus, college sector choice (and employment status) is taken into account in the predictions.[36] The predicted percentage differential for each individual was calculated by:

$$[\exp(\widehat{LNWAGE}_H + .5\text{var}\{\widehat{v_H}\})/\exp(\widehat{LNWAGE}_O$$
$$+ .5\text{var}\{\widehat{v_O}\})] - 1. \qquad (4.15)$$

The predicted percentage differential was then averaged across individuals, by sector.

Hourly wage equations that used data pooled across individuals in both sectors were also estimated; HBI was first treated as exogenous, and then as endogenous:

$$LNWAGE^*_{wi} = X_i\gamma_w + \delta_w I_{1i} + v_{wi}. \qquad (4.16)$$

$LNWAGE^*_w$ is observed if $I_2 = 1$ (i.e., the individual is employed) and not observed if $I_2 = 0$. The procedure for estimating equation 4.16 is similar to that described above for equations 4.8 and 4.9, and the Heckman (1979) method was again utilized. As in equation 4.6, $I_1 = 1$ if an individual attended an HBI, and $I_1 = 0$ otherwise; an instrument for I_1 was obtained through estimation of equation 4.2, which is described in the first section of this appendix.

OCCUPATIONAL STATUS EQUATIONS

The methodology for estimating the occupational status equations, by college sector and for the pooled sample, is the same as that described in the previous section. The only difference is in the way that the average percentage occupational status differential between HBI and non-HBI college attendance (analogous to equation 4.15) was computed. Unlike the wage equation, where the dependent variable is a logarithm, the dependent variable in the status equation is an index. Hence, for occupational status the following was calculated for each individual:

$$(\widehat{SEI79}_H/\widehat{SEI79}_O) - 1. \qquad (4.17)$$

This was then averaged across individuals, by sector.

Notes

Chapter 1

1. See, for example, the discussion in the Carnegie Forum (1986) report calling for significant increases in teacher salaries, justified in part by the comparison of SAT scores of college-bound students. Similar analyses of prospective teachers employing the ACT test are found in Weaver (1983), although that study acknowledges possible supply changes during undergraduate schooling.

2. A separate part of the HSB data collection obtained information on students who were sophomores in 1980, but this panel is not used here.

3. See the overall description of such studies and summary of results in Hanushek (1986, 1989). The studies finding a positive and significant relationship between teacher test score and student performance number eight out of thirty-one separate estimates; another ten studies find positive, but insignificant, effects of teacher test scores. More recent work not surveyed also shows mixed results; cf. Ferguson (1991) and Hanushek (1992).

4. In all cases, the descriptive statistics are weighted according to the sample weights provided in the HSB data. This weighting is important because the HSB data were not derived from a representative national sample but, instead, oversampled certain types of schools and student types.

5. Note, however, that those aspiring to a teaching career in high school are still much more likely than the remaining population to prepare for teaching. Specifically, the portion of the HSB sample that we employ includes 4,509 students who attended some academic postsecondary schooling by the first follow-up in spring 1982.

6. This larger number of people teaching presumably reflects both varying certification requirements and waivers of preparation requirements, either temporary waivers or those included in alternative certification arrangements.

7. Note, again, that the left half of Table 1.1 includes an almost fixed population—those originally aspiring to a teaching career. (A few people exit from school or from teacher training in 1982 and reenter later.) Therefore, ignoring reentrants, as this group is traced over time, a rising mean (or portion in the top of the distribution) comes from people lower in the distribution exiting.

8. To do this analysis, we combine High School and Beyond data with information on state certification requirements found in Woellner (1982) and Goertz, Ekstrom, and Coley (1984). Because the HSB does not provide direct information on state of residence for students, we employ the Hanushek and Taylor (1990) algorithm to determine state of residence.

9. Hanushek (1989) provides evidence that the currently offered graduate training for teachers is quite ineffective. There is little or no evidence suggesting that teachers with advanced training do better in the classroom than those with just a bachelor's degree.

10. Murnane et al. (1991) provide evidence that the stringency of the cutoff score employed has important effects on supply. Thus, the measurement of just the use of such a test is a very crude indication of the importance of this factor across states and over time. See Strauss (1994) for a policy discussion in Pennsylvania.

CHAPTER 2

1. We realize that there may be instances of shared responsibility that will make the use of our definition problematic, but for now we shall assume that at any instant in time one teacher can be identified as the proximate teacher.

2. The specialization might be focused on a domain of knowledge within a curriculum (e.g., mathematics or English), or it might involve an age-grouping of students (e.g., fifth-grade students). The focus might also be on a particular pedagogical style or philosophy (e.g., the Montessori approach). These bounds on specialization can be narrowly or broadly drawn.

3. See Monk (1984) for more on economic aspects of decisions teachers make about the allocation of their time across individual students as well as across groups of students within classes.

4. In the short run, the teacher makes decisions about how much effort to devote to teaching. In the long run, decisions are made about the acquisition of additional training.

5. In an earlier draft of this paper, we paid more explicit attention to what might affect the ability of teachers to utilize the available supply of help from colleagues. One of the interesting results was that much depends on how the "help-needing" (or -seeking) teacher compares with his or her peers. For example, it was not possible to derive the effects of increases in the variance among members of a department on the availability of assistance to a teacher without knowing the individual teacher's placement within the distribution of the relevant attribute.

6. Ehrenberg and Brewer (Forthcoming) recently reanalyzed the EEO data using modern statistical techniques and confirmed the earlier findings regarding the positive independent effects of teachers' verbal ability on pupil performance.

7. Two teachers may have the same score on the test in the data used by Hanushek and his colleagues. In one case, the teacher might be quite bright but might have spent relatively little time learning the subject; in the other case, the teacher might be a very slow learner but might have spent relatively large amounts of time trying to grasp the subject in question.

8. The LSAY data set includes a second cohort that covers a longer period of time. However, these data cover the transition between middle and secondary schools. We chose the secondary student cohort despite the shorter amount of time that is covered because of our interest in the school level of analysis. Work in progress is focused on transitions across schools (King Rice n.d.).

9. For the sophomore analyses, the amount of variation in mathematics gain scores lying within the schools was 94 percent. For the junior year analyses, the proportion lying within the schools was 97 percent.

10. This method yields regression coefficients that are identical to those produced by the more conventional model where a pretest score is used to

predict the posttest result, with the exception of the pretest coefficient. Use of the gain score, rather than the posttest score, as the outcome variable provides desirable information about the relationship between a pupil's starting point and subsequent gains during the period.

11. See, for example, Ehrenberg and Brewer (1994).

12. We classified general or introductory courses in both subjects as remedial (e.g., basic, vocational, and consumer mathematics). In contrast, we classified any mathematics or science course labeled "honors" or "advanced" as advanced.

13. The exception is the two-year-gain model where only the sophomore-year teacher attributes are entered.

14. We also found that the inclusion of these students in the analyses did not generate substantively different results.

CHAPTER 3

1. Quoted in Brint and Karabel (1989), v.

2. *Digest of Education Statistics* (1988), 182.

3. Enrollment figures are from the *Digest of Education Statistics* (1989), 159, 174.

4. The definition of "junior college" is a bit ambiguous. In *The American Junior College,* Cohen and Brawer (1982) define it as ". . . any institution accredited to award the associate's in arts or science as its highest degree" (5–6). This definition includes comprehensive two-year colleges and many technical institutes (both private and public), and it excludes publicly funded vocational schools, adult education centers, and most proprietary schools. Given the changing nature of two-year institutions, however, this definition may not suffice for long. In 1970, associate's degrees comprised about 60 percent of the degrees conferred by junior colleges. By the end of the decade, that proportion had fallen to 40 percent. (Brint and Karabel 1989, 117). I use the terms "community college," "junior college," and "two-year college" interchangeably.

5. Weiss (1992), A1, B10.

6. See Kane and Rouse (1993) for returns to community colleges and Rouse (1993) for the effects on educational attainment.

7. For those familiar with the literature on multinomial logits, I estimate a hybrid of a so-called mother logit and a McFadden (conditional) logit. However, in the usual McFadden logit, utility would be defined as $U_{ij} = \beta_{ij}X + \delta T_{ij}$. I do not constrain δ to have the same impact across all alternatives.

8. The assumption of the independence of irrelevant alternatives associated with the multinomial logit is well documented and means that even if two of the choices are close substitutes, the multinomial logit nonetheless imposes independence. See Hausman and Wise (1978) or Maddala (1983) for more in-depth discussions of the multinomial logit.

9. *Digest of Education Statistics* (1991), 196.

10. *Digest of Education Statistics* (1989), 178.

11. While the junior college literature is full of people noting that junior college students live at home, I have yet to see a reliable estimate.

12. *Fall Enrollment in Colleges and Universities* (1983), 65.

13. *Digest of Education Statistics* (1990), 284.

14. I attempted to estimate the model with state dummies, thereby identifying effects from changes in tuition over time within each state. However, regressing tuition on state dummies reveals that over 95 percent of the variation in tuition is between states over the time period considered here.

15. By classifying people according to the first college attended, I miss the fact that some will attend their first college for only a short period of time before transferring schools. In addition, some attend junior college before they intend to attend college—in other words, before they graduate high school, in the form of summer school. For instance, one famous economist is noted for having studied dinosaurs when seven years old at a local junior college. This problem is mitigated by the fact that I look at the first college attended between the ages of seventeen and nineteen.

16. Actually, many junior colleges are open to those without high school degrees or equivalency diplomas. In the NLSY, only about eight people who had not completed twelve years of school reported having attended a junior college. I suspect that this underestimates the actual use of junior colleges by those without high school degrees and is due to the way in which years of education are recorded in the survey.

17. Pincus (1980), 334.

18. I also estimated the model including the first college attended between the ages of fifteen and thirty-one. The results are substantively the same.

19. The test was administered in 1979. For most of my estimations I include only those who turned eighteen after 1979, which somewhat mitigates the problem that some people will have taken the exam after having attended college. When I estimate the binary decision of whether or not to attend college using an age-adjusted measure of ability (adjusted by regressing ability on dummies for age-at-test and using the residuals), the coefficient on the test score hardly changes.

20. The local unemployment rate in the NLSY is the continuous unemployment rate from the geocode file. The unemployment rate is for the Standard Metropolitan Statistical Area (SMSA) if the individual lived in one, otherwise it is the unemployment rate from the balance (non-SMSA areas) of the state.

21. The wage data are calculated from the Bureau of Labor Statistics Annual Merge file of the CPS for years 1979–88. The experience-adjusted wage differentials are the coefficients on education dummies generated by regressing log wages on a constant, education, and a quartic in potential experience (age-education-6) and estimated separately by race for men and women in each of four regions. The sample included full-time workers under the age of seventy whose major activity the week before was working, who were not self-employed, and who earned at least one-half of the minimum wage.

22. Differences may be explained by the fact that the HSB represents decisions of one cohort within six years after high school, while the NLSY contains several cohorts, the oldest of which attended colleges at age twenty-eight. Also, the NLSY respondents self-reported their type of institution, and some may have included vocational or technical schools with the two-year colleges.

23. A table with results from a binary logit from the NLSY and the HSB are available from the author upon request.

24. To test for the statistical significance of the difference in the effects of independent variables on the choice of two- and four-year college, I tested whether the difference of two variables was statistically different from zero.

25. In ongoing work, Behrman, Kletzer, McPherson, and Schapiro (1992) are also studying the decision to attend both two- and four-year college using the NLS72. While their primary focus is on understanding which family background measures directly affect the decision to attend college (versus indirectly through measured ability), their results are mixed as to the importance of four-year college tuition. However, they use four-year college tuition as a proxy for both four-year and two-year college costs.

26. Also using the SCOPE survey, Radner and Miller (1975) report a nonlinear interaction between measured ability and family resources in predicting college attendance. Among high school seniors with measured ability above the median for the U.S. population, ability to pay (as measured by net cost to the family) was positively related to college attendance, while for those with measured ability below the median for the U.S. population, ability to pay was negatively related to college attendance.

27. I arrived at $2,600 by taking the real expected lifetime earnings of all males starting from age eighteen (to age sixty-four) who were high school graduates, under the assumption of a discount rate of 3 and a 1 percent productivity growth from the *Statistical Abstract,* (U.S. Bureau of the Census 1982) Table 725. I then multiplied this lifetime earnings of $531,000 by 0.005 (the increase in returns I wanted to simulate) to arrive at (about) $2,600.

28. The CPS changed its allocation of students to two-year and four-year colleges in 1987 and 1988. In fact, when I exclude 1987 and 1988 from the weighted regression, the coefficient on relative tuition is 0.01 with a standard error of 0.69.

CHAPTER 4

1. See Christy and Williamson (1992), Fleming (1981), Hill (1984), Hoffman, et al. (1992), and Mingle (1981) for more complete discussions of the formation and history of HBIs.

2. Many of these are vividly described in Rowan (1993).

3. Noteworthy studies include Allen (1986), Allen and Wallace (1988), Anderson and Hoabowsk (1977), Astin (1978), Ayres (1983), Baratz and Ficklen (1983), Cross and Astin (1981), Davis (1988), Fleming (1982, 1984), Pascarella et al. (1987), Pascarella, Smart, and Stoecker (1989), Peterson et al. (1979), Stoecker, Pascarella, and Wolfe (1988), Thomas and Braddock (1981), Thomas (1981), and Thomas and Gordon (1985).

4. In later years, when black students became more common on white campuses, the effects of attendance at an HBI may have changed. As such, in future research we will present similar analyses for black students who entered college in the early 1980s, using data from the High School and Beyond survey.

5. Over 95 percent of undergraduate enrollments in HBIs are in four-year institutions. Hence, the restriction of the sample to students initially in four-year institutions is not a major one. Eighty-one percent of both the HBI sample and other college sample were first enrolled in September 1972 and roughly 10 percent of both first enrolled in each of the next two years, so using a three-year "entrance window" should not cause any problems either.

6. Of the 298 students ever enrolled in an HBI, 253 were enrolled only in HBIs; 12 started in other institutions and shifted to an HBI, while 30 started at an HBI but shifted to another institution. Another 2 students started at HBIs and moved to other institutions, with a spell at an HBI sandwiched in between. In future work, we will analyze the behavior of individuals who changed institutional type.

7. Data on the proportion of black faculty at each American college and university have been collected every few years since 1976 by the Equal Employment Opportunity Commission (EEOC) as part of its Higher Education Staff Information survey. Citing confidentiality and budgetary restrictions, the EEOC formally declined to provide us with data from the early years of the survey. Data for 1989 had been provided to the U.S. Department of Education, however, and

the department kindly permitted us access to a version in which confidential data (earnings) had been removed.

The use of 1989 racial composition of the faculty data obviously provides us with an estimate of the racial composition of the faculty in the 1970s that contains considerable measurement error. As such, this reduces our likelihood of observing that this variable significantly influenced the outcomes of black students.

8. The index of occupational prestige is the revised Duncan index and is found in Featherman and Stevens (1982). The index is defined at the three-digit census occupation level and spans the range from 14.3 to 87.4 in our sample. Prior research has established that this index is highly correlated with the national median earnings and median education levels of individuals employed in the occupation.

9. As Table 4.4 also indicates, these percentages declined by 1988. This mirrors a national trend in which, faced with a declining applicant pool, more and more institutions recruited their students from wider geographic markets.

10. The appendix spells out the formal statistical models used here and throughout the chapter.

11. SLOTS is zero if no HBIs were present in the state.

12. For example, as indicated in Table 4.2, the standard deviations of the proportions of black students and black faculty at HBIs that students in the sample attended were .106 and .131, respectively.

13. For simplicity, we treat whether an individual enrolled in an HBI as given here. This factor could be made endogenous, as it is later in the paper, or determined simultaneously with the other characteristics.

14. Recall the earlier discussion about the high correlation of these variables in the non-HBI sector.

15. See the appendix for details.

16. Similar calculations using the separate sample estimates, which we report below, yield similar findings. We note that in specifications not reported here we found no evidence that the effects of HBIs on bachelor's degree attainment were larger for students who had low test scores or came from low-income families.

17. See the appendix for details.

18. Again, see the appendix for details. The employment status equations included all of the variables that entered into the earnings equations, as well as variables reflecting the individual's marital status, number of children, and (if married) spouse's income—all in 1979. Each of these latter variables' effects were allowed to differ for men and women.

19. Furthermore, in specifications not reported here, we found no evidence that attendance at an HBI was associated with increased 1979 earnings for either students who had low test scores or students from low-income families.

20. Again, as in the previous note, no unique gains were observed for students from low-income families or students with low test scores who attended HBIs.

21. Again, see the appendix for details.

22. In addition, 1979 was no more than three years past college graduation; Labor market outcomes this early may not be good measures of the students' career labor market success. In future work, we plan to use data from the 1986 wave of the NLS72 to address this issue.

23. We have replicated much of the analyses reported in this section, restricting our sample to those students who graduated from high school in states with HBIs. On balance, we found a very similar pattern of results: Attendance at an HBI enhances graduate probabilities but has no impact on early career earnings, occupational status, or the probability of being enrolled in graduate school.

24. Howard University is classified throughout this section as an HBI, not as a Research I institution, which, in fact, it also is.

25. The two percentages are, respectively, for doctorates from HBIs 58 and 4, and for doctorates from Research I institutions 18 and 31.

26. Similarly, the two percentages are, respectively, 41 and 14, and 12 and 36.

27. For example, some federal funding for selected graduate programs at sixteen HBIs in science, engineering, mathematics, and professional fields is provided in fields in which African Americans are underrepresented under Section 303 of PL102-325, the Higher Education Amendment of 1992.

28. The last wave of the NLS72 was conducted in 1986. Unfortunately, the sample size was substantially reduced, which decreases the likelihood that we will be able to observe HBIs having any statistically significant effects in this data set.

29. HSB initially surveyed students who were high school seniors and sophomores in 1980. The former were last resurveyed in 1986 (six years after high school graduation) and the latter in 1992 (ten years after high school graduation). So again, at best, one can focus on early career labor market and educational success with them.

30. This does not take into account the decision of college sector, and future research may utilize a bivariate probit model to incorporate the college sector choice.

31. *LNWAGE* is only partially observable; its observance in each equation depends on sector choice.

32. This technique (using the switching regression model) was applied in an education setting by Willis and Rosen (1979).

33. An individual is counted as not being employed if he or she is not doing market work or is in school full-time.

34. These four outcomes are: (1) HBI and employed; (2) HBI and not employed; (3) non-HBI and employed; (4) non-HBI and not employed.

35. If the disturbance terms in the decision equations are correlated, then a bivariate probit is necessary for estimation.

36. In other words, for those who attended an HBI we are calculating $E(LNWAGE^*_{Hi} \mid X_i, W_{Hi}, I_{1i} = 1, I_{2i} = 1)$ and $E(LNWAGE^*_{Oi} \mid X_i, W_{Oi}, I_{1i} = 1, I_{2i} = 1)$.

Bibliography

Adelman, Clifford A. 1990. "Using Transcripts to Validate an Institutional Mission: The Role of Community Colleges in the Post-secondary Experience of a Generation." U.S. Department of Education, Working Paper OR 90–523. February.

Allen, Walter. 1986. *Gender and Campus Race Differences in Black Student Academic Performance, Racial Attitudes, and College Satisfaction*. Atlanta, Ga.: Southern Educational Foundation. March.

Allen, Walter, and John Wallace. 1988. "Black Students in Higher Education: Correlates of Access Adjustment and Achievement." Paper presented at the annual meeting of the Association for the Study of Higher Education, St. Louis, Mo. November.

Anderson, Ernest F., and Freeman A. Hoabowsk. 1972. "Graduate School Success of Black Students from White Colleges and Black Colleges." *Journal of Higher Education* 47 (May/June): 294–303.

Astin, Alexander E. 1971. *Predicting Academic Performance in College*. New York: Free Press.

———. 1978. *Preventing Students from Dropping Out*. San Francisco, Calif.: Jossey-Bass.

Ayres, Q. Whitfield. 1983. "Student Achievement at Predominantly White and Predominantly Black Universities." *American Educational Research Journal* 20 (2): 291–301.

Baratz, Joan C., and Myra Ficklen. 1983. "Participation of Recent Black College Graduates in Labor Market and Graduate Education." Washington, D.C.: Educational Testing Service.

Barr, Rebecca, and Robert Dreeben. 1983. *How Schools Work*. Chicago: University of Chicago Press.

Behrman, Jere R., et al. 1992. "The College Investment Decision: Direct and Indirect Effects of Family Background on Choice of Post-secondary Enrollment and Quality." Unpublished.

Bidwell, Charles E., and John D. Kasarda. 1975. "School District Organization and Student Achievement." *American Sociological Review* 40: 55–70.

Boe, Erling E. and Dorothy M. Gilford, eds. 1992. *Teacher Supply, Demand, and Quality: Policy Issues, Models, and Data Bases*. Washington, D.C.: National Academy Press.

Bowen, William G. and Neil L. Rudenstine. 1992. *In Pursuit of the Ph.D.* Princeton, N.J.: Princeton University Press.

Breneman, David, and Susan C. Nelson. 1982. *Financing Community Colleges: An Economic Perspective*. Washington, D.C.: The Brookings Institution.

Brint, Steven, and Jerome Karabel. 1989. *The Diverted Dream: Community Colleges and the Promise of Educational Opportunity in America, 1900–1985.* New York: Oxford University Press.

Brown, Byron, and Daniel H. Saks. 1987. "The Microeconomics of the Allocation of Teachers' Time and Student Learning." *Economics of Education Review* 6 (4): 319–32.

Bryk, Anthony S., and Mary E. Driscoll. 1988. *The School as Community: Theoretical Foundations, Contextual Influences, and Consequences for Students and Teachers.* Madison, Wis.: National Center on Effective Secondary Schools.

Bryk, Anthony S., and Stephen W. Raudenbush. 1992. *Hierarchical Linear Models: Applications and Data Analysis Methods.* Newbury Park, Calif.: Sage Publications.

Cameron, Stephen V., and James J. Heckman. 1992. "The Dynamics of Educational Attainment for Blacks, Whites, and Hispanics." University of Chicago. Mimeographed.

Carnegie Forum on Education and the Economy. 1986. *A Nation Prepared: Teachers for the Twenty-First Century.* New York: Carnegie Forum on Education and the Economy.

Chira, Susan. 1992. "Ruling May Force Changes at Southern Universities." *New York Times,* June 27, 10.

Christy, Ralph D., and Lionel Williamson, eds. 1992. *A Century of Service.* New Brunswick, N.J.: Transaction Publishers.

Clark, Burton R. 1960. "The 'Cooling-Out' Function in Higher Education." *American Journal of Sociology* 65 (6): 569–76.

Clotfelter, Charles T., et al. 1991. *Economic Challenges in Higher Education.* Chicago: University of Chicago Press.

Cohen, Arthur M., and Florence B. Brawer. 1982. *The American Community College.* San Francisco, Calif.: Jossey-Bass.

Coleman, James S., et al. 1966. *Equality of Educational Opportunity.* Washington, D.C.: U.S. Department of Health, Education, and Welfare.

Cross, K., and H. Astin. 1981. "Factors Influencing Black Students' Persistence in College." In *Black Students in Higher Education,* edited by Gail E. Thomas. Westport, Conn.: Greenwood Press.

Davis, James E. 1988. "Differential Academic Progression of Black Students at Historically Black Public and Private Colleges and Universities." Ph.D. diss., Cornell University, Ithaca, N.Y.

Digest of Education Statistics. 1987, 1989, 1990, 1991. Washington, D.C.: U.S. Department of Health, Education, and Welfare, Education Division, National Center for Education Statistics.

Dougherty, Kevin. 1987. "The Effects of Community Colleges: Aid or Hindrance to Socioeconomic Attainment?" *Sociology of Education* 60: 86–103.

Dreeben, Robert, and Rebecca Barr. 1988. "The Formation and Instruction of Ability Groups." *American Journal of Education* 97 (1): 34–64.

Ehrenberg, Ronald G. 1992. "The Flow of New Doctorates." *Journal of Economic Literature* 30 (June): 830–75.

Ehrenberg, Ronald, and Dominic Brewer. Forthcoming. "Did Teachers' Verbal Ability and Race Matter in the 1960s? Coleman Revisited." *Economics of Education Review.*

———. 1994. "Do School and Teacher Characteristics Matter?: Evidence from High School and Beyond." *Economics of Education Review* 13 (1):1–18.

Fall Enrollment in Colleges and Universities. 1983. Washington, D.C.: National Center for Education Statistics.

Featherman, David L., and Gillian Stevens. 1982. "A Revised Socioeconomic Indicator of Occupational Status." In *Social Structure and Behavior*, edited by Robert Hauser, et al. New York: Academic Press.

Ferguson, Ronald F. 1991. "Paying for Public Education: New Evidence on How and Why Money Matters." *Harvard Journal on Legislation* 28 (2): 465–98.

Fleming, Jacqueline. 1982. "Sex Differences in the Impact of College Environments on Black Students." In *The Undergraduate Woman: Issues in Educational Equity*, edited by Pamela Perun. Lexington, Mass.: D. C. Heath.

———. 1984. *Blacks in College: A Comparative Study of Students' Success in Black and White Institutions*. San Francisco, Calif.: Jossey-Bass.

Fleming, John E. 1981. "Blacks in Higher Education to 1954: A Historical Overview." In *Black Students in Higher Education*, edited by Gail E. Thomas. Westport, Conn.: Greenwood Press.

Gamoran, Adam. 1987. "The Stratification of High School Learning Opportunities." *Sociology of Education* 60: 135–55.

Goertz, Margaret E., Ruth B. Ekstrom, and Richard J. Coley. 1984. "The Impact of State Policy on Entrance into the Teaching Profession: Final Report." Princeton, N.J.: Educational Testing Service. October. Mimeographed.

Grubb, W. Norton. 1988. "Vocationalizing Higher Education: The Causes of Enrollment and Completion in Public Two-Year Colleges, 1979–1980." *Economics of Education Review* 7 (3): 301–19.

———. 1989. "The Effects of Differentiation on Educational Attainment: The Case of Community Colleges." *Review of Higher Education* 12: 349–74.

———. 1991. "The Varied Economic Returns to Post-secondary Education: New Evidence from the National Longitudinal Study of the Class of 1972." University of California, Berkeley. Mimeographed.

Guilford, Dorothy, and Ellen Tenenbaum, eds. 1990. *Precollege Science and Mathematics Teachers: Monitoring Supply, Demand, and Quality*. Washington, D.C.: National Academy Press.

Hallinan, Maureen T., and Aage B. Sorensen. 1985. "Class Size, Ability Group Size, and Student Achievement." *American Journal of Education* 94 (1): 71–89.

Hanushek, Eric A. 1986. "The Economics of Schooling: Production and Efficiency in Public Schools." *Journal of Economic Literature* 24 (3): 1141–77.

———. 1989. "The Impact of Differential Expenditures on School Performance." *Educational Researcher* 18 (4): 45–51.

———. 1992. "The Trade-Off between Child Quantity and Quality." *Journal of Political Economy* 100 (1) (February): 84–117.

Hanushek, Eric A., and Lori Taylor. 1990. "Alternative Assessments of the Performance of Schools: Measurement of State Variations in Achievement." *Journal of Human Resources* 25 (2): 179–201.

Hanushek, Eric A., Joao Batista Gomes-Neto, and Ralph W. Harbison. 1992. "Self-Financing Educational Investments: The Quality Imperative in Developing Countries." University of Rochester. Mimeographed.

Hanushek, Eric A., Steven G. Rivkin and Dean T. Jamison. 1992. "Improving Educational Outcomes while Controlling Costs." *Carnegie-Rochester Conference Series on Public Policy* 37 (December): 205–38.

Hausman, Jerry A., and David A. Wise. "A Conditional Probit Model for Qualitative Choice: Discrete Decisions Recognizing Interdependence and Heterogeneous Preferences." *Econometrica* 46, no. 2 (March 1978): 403–26.

Heckman, James. 1979. "Sample Bias as a Specification Error." *Econometrica* 47 (January): 153–62.

Hill, Susan T. 1984. *The Traditionally Black Institutions of Higher Education: 1860 to 1982*. Washington, D.C.: National Center for Education Statistics.

Hoffman, Charlene M., et al. 1992. *Historically Black Colleges and Universities, 1976–90.* Washington, D.C.: National Center for Education Statistics.

Holmes Group. 1986. *Tomorrow's Teachers.* East Lansing, Mich.: The Holmes Group.

James, Estelle, et al. 1989. "College Quality and Future Earnings: Where Should You Send Your Children to College?" *American Economic Association Papers and Proceedings* 79 (May): 247–52.

Johnson, Julie. 1991. "Are Black Colleges Worth Saving?" *Time*, November 11: 81–83.

Johnson, Susan M. 1990. *Teachers at Work: Achieving Success in Our Schools.* New York: Basic Books.

Kane, Thomas J. 1991. "College Entry by Blacks since 1970: The Role of Tuition, Financial Aid, Local Economic Conditions, and Family Background." Ph.D. diss., Harvard University, Cambridge, Mass.

Kane, Thomas J., and Cecilia Elena Rouse. 1993. "Labor Market Returns to Two- and Four-Year Colleges: Is a Credit a Credit and Do Degrees Matter?" Cambridge, Mass.: NBER, Working Paper No. 4268. January.

King Rice, Jennifer A. n.d. "The Effects of Transitions across Schools on Student Performance in Mathematics and Science." Ph.D. diss. in progress, Cornell University, Ithaca, N.Y.

Kohn, Meir G., Charles F. Manski, and David S. Mundel. 1976. "An Empirical Investigation of Factors Influencing College-Going Behavior." *Annals of Economic and Social Measurement* 5: 391–419.

Leslie, Larry L., and Paul T. Brinkman. 1988. *The Economic Value of Higher Education.* New York: American Council on Education, Macmillan.

Maddala, G. S. 1983. *Limited-Dependent and Qualitative Variables in Econometrics.* New York: Cambridge University Press.

Manski, Charles F. 1987. "Academic Ability, Earnings, and the Decision to Become a Teacher: Evidence from the National Longitudinal Study of the High School Class of 1972." In *Public Sector Payrolls*, edited by David A. Wise. Chicago: University of Chicago Press.

Manski, Charles F., and David A. Wise. 1983. *College Choice in America.* Cambridge: Harvard University Press.

McPherson, Michael S., and Morton Owen Schapiro. 1991. "Does Student Aid Affect College Enrollment? New Evidence on a Persistent Controversy." *American Economic Review* 81 (1): 309–18.

Millman, Jason, and Gary Sykes. 1992. "The Assessment of Teaching Based on Evidence of Student Learning: An Analysis." Paper prepared for the National Board for Professional Teaching Standards.

Mingle, James R. 1981. "The Opening of White Colleges and Universities to Black Students." In *Black Students in Higher Education*, edited by Gail E. Thomas. Westport, Conn.: Greenwood Press.

Monk, David H. 1984. "Interdependencies among Educational Inputs and Resource Allocation in Classrooms." *Economics of Education Review* 3 (1): 65–73.

———. 1994. "The Content Preparation of Secondary Mathematics and Science Teachers and Pupil Achievement." *Economics of Education Review.*

———. 1994. "Subject Area Preparation of Secondary Mathematics and Science Teachers and Student Achievement." *Economics of Education Review* 13 (2): 125–45.

Monk, David H., and Emil J. Haller. 1993. "Predictors of High School Academic Course Offerings: The Role of School Size." *American Educational Research Journal* 30 (1): 3–21.

Murnane, Richard, et al. 1991. *Who Will Teach? Policies That Matter.* Cambridge: Harvard University Press.

National Center for Education Statistics (NCES). 1992. *Digest of Education Statistics, 1992.* Washinton, D.C.: U.S. Department of Education.

Odden, Allan, and Sharon Conley. 1991. "Restructuring Teacher Compensation Systems to Foster Collegiality and Help Accomplish National Education Goals." University of Southern California. Mimeographed.

Pascarella, Ernst T., et al. 1987. "The Influence of College on Self-Concept: A Reconsideration of Race and Gender Differentials." *American Education Research Journal* 24: 49–77.

Pascarella, Ernst T., John C. Smart, and Judith Stoecker. 1989. "College Race and the Early Status Attainment of Black Students." *Journal of Higher Education* 60: 82–107.

Pascarella, Ernst T., and Patrick T. Terenzini. 1991. *How College Affects Students: Findings and Insights from Twenty Years of Research.* San Francisco, Calif.: Jossey-Bass.

Peterson, Marvin W., et al. 1979. *Black Students on White Campuses: The Impacts of Increased Black Enrollments.* Ann Arbor: University of Michigan Institute for Social Research.

Pincus, Fred L. 1980. "The False Promises of Community Colleges: Class Conflict and Vocational Education." *Harvard Educational Review* 50: 332–61.

Radner, Roy, and Leonard S. Miller. 1975. *Demand and Supply in U.S. Higher Education.* Report prepared for the Carnegie Commission on Higher Education, New York: McGraw-Hill.

Rouse, Cecilia Elena. 1993. "Democratization or Diversion? The Effect of Community Colleges on Educational Attainment." Princeton, N.J.: Industrial Relations Section, Working Paper No. 313.

Rowan, Brian, Stephen W. Raudenbush, and Sang Jin Kang. 1991. "Organizational Design in High Schools: A Multilevel Analysis." *American Journal of Education* 99 (2): 238–70.

Rowan, Carl. 1993. *Breaking Barriers: A Memoir.* Boston: Little, Brown.

Stoecker, Judith, Ernst T. Pascarella, and Lee M. Wolfe. 1988. "Persistence in Higher Education: A Nine-Year Test of the Theoretical Model." *Journal of College Student Development* 29: 196–209.

Strauss, Robert P. 1993. "Public School Teachers in Pennsylvania: Demand and Supply through School Year 2000." Pittsburgh, Pa.: Carnegie Melon University. Mimeographed.

———. 1994. "Teacher Certification Tests and the Personnel Decision." Pennsylvania School Boards Association, Education Management Guidelines (April): 1–3.

Summers, Anita, and Barbara Wolfe. 1977. "Do Schools Make a Difference?" *American Economic Review* 67 (4): 639–52.

Thomas, Gail E. 1981. "College Characteristics and Black Students' Four-Year College Graduation." *Journal of Negro Education* 50: 328–45.

Thomas, Gail E., and Jomills H. Braddock II. 1981. *Determining the College Destination of Black Students.* Atlanta: Southern Educational Foundation.

Thomas, Gail E., and Samuel A. Gordon. 1985. *Evaluating the Payoffs of College Investments for Black, White, and Hispanic Students.* Baltimore: Johns Hopkins University Center for Social Organizations of Schools, Report No. 344.

Tinto, Vincent. 1973. "College Proximity and Rates of College Attendance." *American Educational Research Journal* 10: 277–93.

U.S. Bureau of the Census. 1982. *Statistical Abstract of the United States: 1982–1983.* 103d ed. Washington, D.C.

———. *Census of Population and Housing,* 1940, 1950, 1960, 1970, 1980, 1990.

U.S. House of Representatives. 1991. Committee on Education and Labor.

Hearing on Issues and Matters Pertaining to Historically Black Colleges and Universities. 101st Congress, 2d sess. Washington, D.C.: GPO.

Weaver, W. Timothy. 1983. *America's Teacher Quality Problem: Alternatives for Reform.* New York: Praeger.

Weiss, Samuel. 1992. "CUNY Tuition Plan: Biggest Increase Yet but a Free Semester." *New York Times*, April 15, 1A.

Willis, Robert J., and Sherwin Rosen. 1979. "Education and Self-Selection." *Journal of Political Economy* 87 (October): S7–S36.

Woellner, Elizabeth H. 1982. *Requirements for Certification, 1982–83.* 47th ed. Chicago: University of Chicago Press.

Zarkin, Gary A. 1985. "Occupational Choice: An Application to the Market for Public School Teachers." *Quarterly Journal of Economics* (May): 409–46.

About the Contributors

Ronald G. Ehrenberg is the Irving M. Ives Professor of Industrial and Labor Relations and Economics at Cornell University, the director of the ILR-Cornell Institute for Labor Market Policies, and a research associate at the National Bureau of Economic Research.

Eric A. Hanushek is a professor of economics and public policy at the University of Rochester and serves as the director of the Wallis Institute of Political Economy.

Jennifer A. King is a researcher at Mathematica Policy Research in Washington, D.C.

David H. Monk is a professor of educational administration at Cornell University.

Richard R. Pace is an assistant professor of economics at the University of Dayton.

Donna S. Rothstein is a Ph.D. candidate in the Department of Labor Economics at Cornell University and received a National Science Foundation doctoral dissertation grant.

Cecilia Elena Rouse is an assistant professor of economics and public affairs at Princeton University and is a faculty research fellow at the National Bureau of Economic Research.